As one of the world's longest established and best-known travel brands, Thomas Cook are the experts in travel.

For more than 135 years our guidebooks have unlocked the secrets of destinations around the world, sharing with travellers a wealth of experience and a passion for travel.

Rely on Thomas Cook as your travelling companion on your next trip and benefit from our unique heritage.

Thomas Cook **traveller** guides

DUBLIN
Conor Caffrey

Thomas Cook

Your travelling companion since 1873

Written by Conor Caffrey, updated by Sean Sheehan
Original photography by Conor Caffrey

Published by Thomas Cook Publishing
A division of Thomas Cook Tour Operations Limited
Company registration no. 3772199 England
The Thomas Cook Business Park, Unit 9, Coningsby Road,
Peterborough PE3 8SB, United Kingdom
Email: books@thomascook.com, Tel: + 44 (0) 1733 416477
www.thomascookpublishing.com

Produced by Cambridge Publishing Management Limited
Burr Elm Court, Main Street, Caldecote CB23 7NU

ISBN: 978-1-84848-230-2

© 2003, 2006, 2008 Thomas Cook Publishing
This fourth edition © 2010
Text © Thomas Cook Publishing
Maps © Thomas Cook Publishing/PCGraphics (UK) Limited
Reproduced from Ordnance Survey Ireland Permit No. 8643
© Ordnance Survey Ireland and Government of Ireland
Transport map © Communicarta Limited

Series Editor: Maisie Fitzpatrick
Production/DTP: Steven Collins

Printed and bound in Italy by Printer Trento

Cover photography: © Art Kowalsky/Alamy

Contents

Introduction

Dublin is the 'fair' city immortalised in song, even though its most famous writer, James Joyce, described it as 'dear dirty Dublin'. It is an endearing city and you will succumb more to its charms the longer you stay. It is not really Dublin's architecture that is so attractive; although there is some elegant Georgian architecture in the city, it does not compare to Paris, Barcelona or Prague. Dublin's museums and galleries are impressive, but they do not match those in Berlin or London.

The great attraction of Dublin is the people and their welcome, warmth and friendliness. The Dubliners will win over your heart and provide you with the impetus to start planning your return visit before you have even left the city.

You may not understand everything a Dubliner says, even though they speak the same language, but if you do understand it then it will probably have been a smile-inducing remark. You are unlikely to meet a more good-natured bunch of people. Dubliners are always willing to give advice, but take their advice with a grain of salt; you might end up going the wrong way if you ask for directions, but at least you will end up seeing a part of the city you may not have otherwise seen.

Dublin is the capital of the emerald isle of Ireland, known as the Land of Saints and Scholars. The city lives up to this reputation although there are, and have been, considerably more scholars than saints within the city boundaries.

The scholars are invariably of the literary variety and it is the strongest aspect of Dublin's heritage. Three of Ireland's four Nobel Prize winners for literature – W B Yeats, George Bernard Shaw and Samuel Beckett – hailed from Dublin. The fourth, Seamus Heaney, has also lived here, and there is a whole host of other famous writers who have gained their inspiration from the characters they meet on the streets and in the pubs of Dublin. The Dubliners were the inspiration for these great writers and, as you wander around the streets of the city centre and eavesdrop on the conversations of the passers-by, you will catch a glimpse of the world that Dublin's writers have exploited, and continue to exploit today. The strange mixture of the language spoken by Dubliners who adapted the English language for their own use, and their peculiarities and quirkiness of character, has led to an inspiration for the great works of Irish writers.

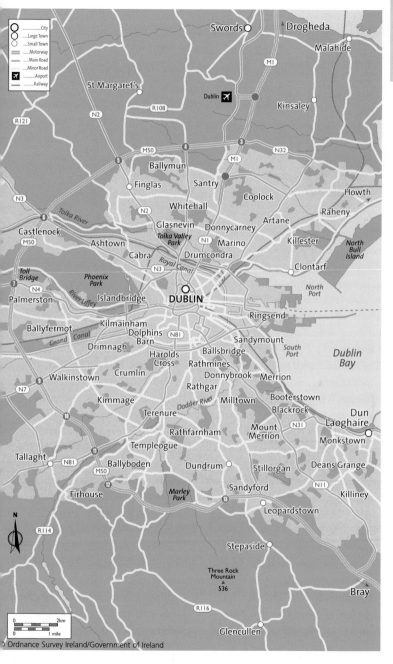

The city

Dublin is situated at 53°20′N of the equator and 6°21′W of the Greenwich Mean. It is found in the marvellousl scenic Dublin Bay, which stretches from Howth Hea down to Sorrento Point in Dalkey. There are nearly 11km (7 miles) between the two as the crow flies. Dublin is abou halfway down the east coast of Ireland.

The population of the city is 506,000, but about 1.6 million people live in the greater Dublin area and within commuting distance of the city centre (within 100km/62 miles). This is about 40 per cent of the national population.

Climate

The Romans called Ireland *Hibernia*, which translates as 'Land of winter'. Although it does sometimes feel that there is rarely any summer in Ireland and every day is grey, you can get good weather at any time of the year. The problem is that it is impossible to predict and it does not necessarily last for any length of time.

The climate of Dublin, as with the whole of Ireland, is affected by the Gulf Stream or the North Atlantic Drift, which flows across the Atlantic Ocean from the Gulf of Mexico. The temperature can be best described as mild; it is rarely colder than 0°C (32°F), with only a handful of days of frost per year, and it is rarely warmer than 20°C (68°F) in the summertime.

No matter how a day starts, it is likel to change. If dark and rainy in the morning, it might clear up and be sunny in the afternoon, and if there are clear skies, it might pour down in the afternoon. For your trip, come prepare for any type of weather. The summer temperatures are generally warmer and drier, but you should be prepared and always expect the unexpected.

The Irish love to talk about the weather and Dubliners are no exception. It is natural to be an expert on the vagaries of the local climate and you are guaranteed to get an opinion o two when you stop to chat to one of th locals. Invariably they will either complain vehemently about it or show a stoicism that is beyond belief when conditions are positively atrocious. The confusing thing is that you may hear such utterances of completely contrasting opinions on the same day and from the same individual!

The city

There is a rather negative local saying that if it is not raining then it is just about to start. Even though this is not always the case, the weather can change so quickly at any time of the year that it is best to plan for it. Bring a raincoat and if you have an umbrella with you, even better.

Areas of Dublin

The River Liffey splits Dublin in two into the Northside centred around O'Connell St and the Southside centred around Grafton St. Although this is the major division of the city centre, there are some small local areas that have

SMOKING IN PUBLIC

As with the UK, visiting smokers to Ireland need to be forewarned that there is a ban on smoking in offices, on all modes of public transport and in bars and restaurants.

The days of the stereotypical image of a smoky Dublin pub on a weekend night heaving with people chatting and a traditional band playing in the corner are over. At least, the smoking aspect is no more.

The legislation implemented at the start of 2005 has largely been accepted now, although some smokers and publicans feel that the ban on smoking in pubs has destroyed that quintessential atmosphere of the Irish pub and has infringed on the smoker's right to smoke. Rural publicans claim they have lost money. A lot of pubs and restaurants have constructed tarpaulin-covered extensions to their premises for smokers and there is now a new vibrant street culture outside many of the city's pubs and bars, as smokers gather for a 'fag and a chat' on the pavement. Non-smokers have embraced the legislation, and feel it hasn't destroyed the atmosphere of the pubs but rather enhanced it.

Georgian streetlamps are one of the city's landmarks

been redeveloped and have taken on their own personality.

On the Southside the Temple Bar area is famous for its nightlife, great bars and restaurants. It is also a cultural centre, with art galleries and the Irish film centre being located in the area.

On the Northside the Docklands is a major commercial centre with modern architecture, chic restaurants and bars catering for financial centre workers with large expendable incomes, although at weekends the area is very quiet.

The suburbs of Dublin stretch in three directions as the city hugs the dramatic Dublin Bay.

The city

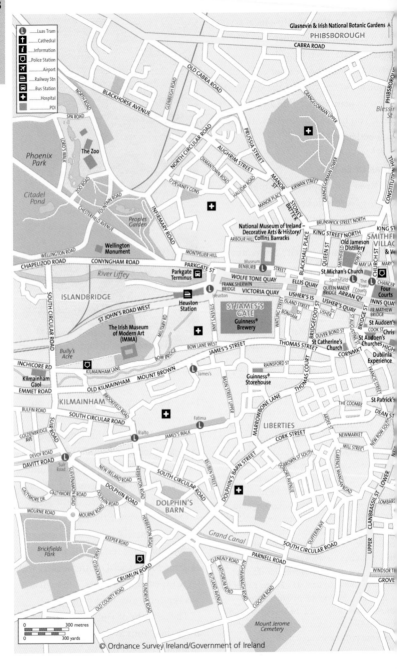

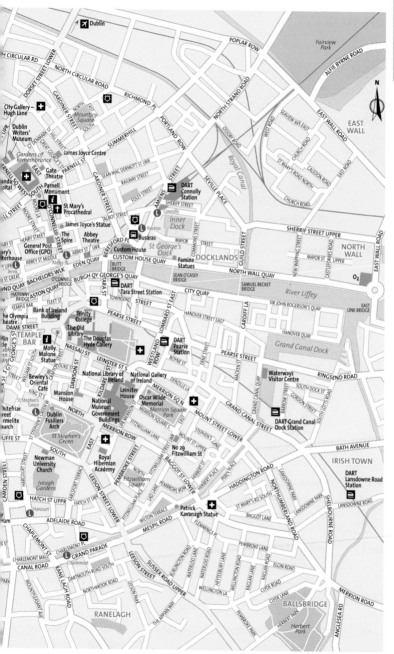

History

5000 BC	Evidence of early habitation in Dublin area.
4000 BC	Neolithic farms.
700 BC	Arrival of the Celts. Establishment of Dublin. Its name, still Gaelic, was *Baile Atha Cliath* or 'Town of the Ford of Hurdles'.
AD 100	Ptolemy's map of Ireland with Eblana roughly in the place where Dublin is now.
432	St Patrick arrived in Ireland. He is said to have baptised people on the site of St Patrick's Cathedral in AD 450.
841	A large Viking fleet overwinters in Dublin. Vikings build first harbour.
919	Battle of Dublin between the Vikings and the King of Tara at Islandbridge.
1014	Battle of Clontarf. Brian Boru defeats Vikings.
1042	St Michan's Church is built.
1169	Strongbow's Norman army invades Ireland.

1191	St Patrick's Cathedral is built.
1197	Dublin excommunicated by the Pope after an argument with King John.
1297	First Irish Parliament meets in Dublin.
1348	Black Death. One-third of the population dies.
1541	Henry VIII declared King of Ireland by the Irish Parliament.
1585	Ireland is mapped and divided into 32 counties.
1592	Trinity College founded.
1649	Cromwell lands in Dublin – razes Drogheda and Wexford.
1690	William of Orange defeats James II at the Battle of the Boyne.
1713	Jonathan Swift appointed Dean of St Patrick's Cathedral.
1731	Royal Dublin Society founded.

1742	Première of Handel's *Messiah* at the Music Hall on Fishamble St.
1751	Rotunda Hospital is opened as the first maternity hospital in Britain and Ireland.
1769	Arthur Guinness starts brewing the world-famous Guinness® stout.
1791	James Gandon builds the Customs House.
1800	The Act of Union. The Irish Parliament votes to disband the Parliament. Ireland legally becomes part of Britain.
1828	Catholic Emancipation Act is passed, giving a vote to a limited number of Irish Catholics.
1845	The Great Famine lasts for three years. About 1 million people die in Ireland from the failure of two successive potato crops. Dublin fills up with starving migrants from the countryside.
1877	Charles Stewart Parnell becomes leader of the Home Rule Party.

1881	Parnell is jailed in Kilmainham Gaol.
1884	Founding of Gaelic Athletic Association.
1891	Funeral of Charles Stewart Parnell with procession through Dublin attended by 200,000 people.
1907	J M Synge's *Playboy of the Western World* opens at the Abbey Theatre.
1913	Irish Volunteers founded. Liverpudlian James 'Big Jim' Larkin leads a strike of unskilled workers who would not join the Irish Transport and General Workers' Union.
1916	Easter Rising.
1918	Sinn Féin wins elections. Countess Markievicz, Sinn Feiner and member of the Anglo-Irish gentry, becomes the first woman to be elected to the British House of Commons.
1921	Signing of Anglo-Irish Treaty.
1922	Assassination of Michael Collins. Independence is won and the Republic

	formed. James Joyce's novel *Ulysses* is published and banned.
1941	German air raid on Dublin during World War II.
1963	US President John F Kennedy visits Ireland.
1966	Nelson's pillar landmark on Sackville St (now O'Connell St) is blown up.
1970	Ban on Catholics attending Trinity College is lifted.
1973	Ireland joins the European Union.
1974	Bomb explosions in Dublin kill 25.
1976	British ambassador to Ireland assassinated.
1979	Pope John Paul II's visit.
1988	Dublin celebrates its millennium.
1990	Mary Robinson elected first woman president.
1991	Dublin is declared European City of Culture.
1995	Divorce made legal in Ireland.

2002	Ireland adopts the Euro as its currency and ratifies the Treaty of Nice.
2004	Ireland assumes EU Presidency.
2005	IRA disarm. End to violence in Northern Ireland.
2007	Bertie Ahern elected Taoiseach for a historic third term.
2008	The world economic crisis hits Ireland badly; several banks teeter on the verge of collapse. Irish voters reject the Treaty of Lisbon, which would create a constitution for Europe at the expense of individual countries' freedoms.
2009	Little sign of economic revival. House prices fall, businesses fail. The Treaty of Lisbon is voted on for a second time – this time, the Irish people vote 'yes'.
2011	The redeveloped Lansdowne Road stadium hosts the final of the UEFA Europa League.

Dublin Castle has a tainted history

Ancient Dublin

Like many primitive populations, the early Irish were nomads and did not form settlements. There is evidence, however, of Neolithic sites in the Boyne Valley not too far from Dublin. But ancient Dublin didn't really get going until the Vikings, and later the Normans, turned up.

The Vikings from Scandinavia are recognised as the city founders. After years of raiding monastic island sites off the coast of Ireland, up to 60 Viking longboats eventually overwintered in Dublin in about AD 841. It is not certain exactly where these first Vikings settled to spend this winter, but it seems they subsequently developed two permanent settlements or *longphorts*, which were ports for their longships.

One of these *longphorts* was at Kilmainham on the site of an ancient monastery. Some early Viking graves were found at Kilmainham and Islandbridge nearby. Some historians believe that here the ancient roads crossed at the ford which gave Dublin its name in Irish – *Baile Atha Cliath* or 'Town of the Ford of Hurdles'. The River Camac joins the River Liffey and would have been a narrow crossing. The second *longphort* site was at Dubh Linn (in Irish) or the 'black pool'. Most people consider this place to be the origin of Dublin. Again it was where two rivers meet; the rivers Poddle and Liffey. In those times the black pool of water would have been quite large. It is also the second proposed site of the Ford of Hurdles. The crossing would have been much wider and shallower than at Islandbridge.

The *longphorts* were used as raiding base camps and the Vikings would go off and pillage monasteries and bring back slaves. The first wave of Viking raiders was from Norway (called the *Fingall* or 'white strangers'), and they were followed by the Danes (called the *Dubhgall* or 'dark strangers'). The

Viking replica ship on the Liffey

two factions started to compete for supremacy. The Irish took advantage of this infighting and drove the Vikings out of Dublin in AD 902. The Vikings returned in 917 and built a proper trading port at Wood Quay. They settled as merchants (introducing coinage to Ireland) and they formed alliances with the Irish, intermarrying and some even converting to Christianity. Viking Dublin fell into decline and the Vikings were eventually defeated by the heroic Brian Boru at the Battle of Clontarf in 1014.

The second great group of invaders that came to ancient Dublin were the Anglo-Normans. They were invited to invade by the cruel Irish chieftain and traitor Dermot McMurrough. The Normans came to Dublin in 1170 led by Richard de Clare, or Strongbow, as he was also known (the first Irish Viceroy), and they captured the city through a mix of deceit and brutality. Yet the Normans also built up the city and were responsible for the construction of the great cathedrals (Christchurch and St Patrick's) and Dublin Castle. Trade flourished and the city population increased, becoming very crowded with narrow medieval streets. The arrival of the Normans marked the beginning of British rule in Ireland, which ended with independence and the formation of the Republic in 1922. Although the

Dublin Castle, on a site originally developed by the Normans

Anglo-Irish were considered British colonists, after a generation or two many of them had become fully integrated into Irish society and equally disillusioned with the forces of the British Crown.

You can catch a flavour of medieval Dublin at **Dublinia**, an experience museum which recreates Dublin's medieval streets and provides information on what life was like. *Dublinia, Synod Hall, Christchurch Pl. Tel: (01) 679 4611. www.dublinia.ie. Open: daily 10am–5pm. Last admission 45 mins before closing. Closed: 23–26 Dec & 17 Mar. Tearooms open: Jun–Aug. Admission charge. Guided tours: daily at 2.30pm.*

Politics

The Republic of Ireland was formed in 1922 when Ireland achieved independence after 700 years of British rule. The country is governed by a parliamentary system called the Oireachtas.

The government

The constitutional head of the government is the President, who is elected for a seven-year term, and resides in Áras an Uachtaráin (House of the President) in Phoenix Park. The current President is Belfast-born Mary McAleese.

The Irish Republic has two houses of parliament. The lower house is the Dáil and this is the House of Representatives. The members of the Dáil Eireann (Irish Parliament) are called TDs, which comes from the Irish *Teachta Dála*, meaning member of the Dáil, like the British MP. The TDs are elected by the general public using a proportional representation voting system. There are 166 elected members of the Dáil, and it sits in Leinster House on Kildare St. The head of the government is called the Taoiseach and the second in command is called the Tánaiste. The current Taoiseach is Brian Cowen from Clara, County Offaly. He is leader of the Fianna Fáil party – the

largest party in the State. His Tánaiste is Mary Coughlan, who is also deputy leader of Fianna Fáil and Minister for Enterprise. The second house is the Senate (*Seanad*), and the senators are nominated by the Taoiseach or elected by university graduates and town councillors nationwide.

Modern Ireland and Europe

In 1973 Ireland joined the European Union and initially benefited greatly from this move, particularly from the Common Agricultural Policy and Regional Development Funds. In the early 1980s emigration rose and the economy struggled. Through a combination of generous tax incentives and the availability of a highly skilled workforce, the Irish economy started to boom in the early 1990s. Ireland had a particularly high number of computer graduates and the IT sector was the cornerstone of the success of the 'Celtic Tiger' economy. This is why many of the biggest computer companies decided to locate their European headquarters in the country. In 2002 Ireland adopted the Euro as its currency and ratified the Nice Treaty at the second attempt. Ireland has become fully integrated in the new Europe.

In 2004 Ireland assumed the Presidency of the EU and it proved to be one of the most successful presidential sessions. During the six-month presidency the EU grew to comprise 25 member states and a draft constitutional treaty was agreed.

In 2008 the Celtic tiger, already a little hoarse, ceased its fearless roar, as the global economic meltdown exposed the weaknesses of a system that gave huge loans to speculative construction projects on the assumption that property prices would continue to rise. Jobs began disappearing, migrant workers turned to other places, and negative equity became a buzzword in the housing market for the first time in Irish history. Dublin's many development projects, particularly those on the north side of the river, began to look less profitable or even impossible. There was further bad news for the city in 2009, as a public enquiry into church-run industrial schools in the last century exposed the extent of the cruelty found in such places, in particular the Dublin Artane Industrial School. In the midst of all this, Ireland suffered the embarrassment of being the only European country not to ratify the Treaty of Lisbon. Its citizens, duly admonished, were ordered to vote in a second referendum in 2009, as if they had somehow arrived at the wrong decision. This time, they voted 'yes'.

The biggest event in Ireland's recent history was in September 2005, when independent weapons inspectors witnessed the disarmament of the IRA, ending the 30-year-long violent campaign in Northern Ireland with positive consequences for Dublin's future as well as those living in the Six Counties of the north.

Leinster House: the seat of the Irish Parliament

Culture and festivals

Dublin is a city defined more by the character of its people than by the stone of its buildings and streets, which may sometimes seem dour and grey. It is a city that is very much alive, and often the noise of human voices conversing is louder than the infamous traffic that fills the streets.

Religion

Religion still plays an important role in Irish life although it is perhaps less important now than it used to be. Many Irish adults were educated by religious orders and, for some of them, their lives have been tainted by the experience. Most Irish people are Roman Catholics. However, many young people do not attend Mass regularly and are considered to be non-practising Catholics. The power of the Church in Ireland has been declining for decades and many feel that it has lost touch not only with its people, but also with reality. Recent scandals about cases of child abuse by priests, ignored for years by the Catholic hierarchy, have done untold damage to the Irish Catholic Church's reputation and alienated churchgoers. However, during the major religious festivals of Easter, and especially Christmas, many non-practising Catholics will attend Mass, and many young people may have a church wedding even if they are not regular churchgoers. Ireland is much more liberal now than when the Church held greater sway, and attitudes to issues such as contraception, abortion and divorce have become more open. Abortion is still banned in the country and a referendum to change the law was defeated.

To some, Catholicism is associated with Nationalism in Ireland, in spite of the fact that in history many Protestants were also Irish nationalists. In the North of Ireland, religion has been exploited by both Nationalist and Unionist communities to reinforce the sectarian divide. This has had the tragic consequence of what Irish people call the 'Troubles' in Ireland.

Multiculturalism

The most significant change in Ireland in recent years, and particularly in Dublin, has been the massive influx of foreign nationals. The majority of recent immigrants have come from Eastern Europe following EU

A float on St Patrick's Day emphasises Dublin's multiculturalism

enlargement in 2004, the most significant number coming from Poland. However, there has also been an influx of people of Asian and African origin, particularly Nigerians.

Ireland has had to adapt from being a monocultural society to a multicultural one in a very short space of time. This has brought with it intrinsic problems, but the ethnic diversity, particularly in cities such as Dublin, has enriched the country's culture. Tolerance is key to the peaceful integration of these immigrants, and for the most part Irish people seem pretty welcoming towards the newcomers, but this has changed Dublin's identity dramatically. Don't be surprised if half the voices you hear on the street aren't Irish ones!

The chat and a story

Don't go to Dublin if you don't want to talk because the city is definitely a place for conversation. If you stand still for an instant you will be engaged in an open-ended discussion by one of the locals, and a Dubliner's conversation embraces any number of topics. Even if you have buried your head well into your map to try to work out exactly where you are, someone is likely to draw you into conversation. The discussion may be about anything at all, from the weather to politics, but the local will try to find out about you, for curiosity is a Dublin trait. It may take you many minutes to get out of it, by which time you may

both have swapped your life stories. But that is all part of the enjoyment of the place.

The Irish, as well as being great conversationalists, are also great storytellers. This is one source of their great literary heritage. The thing to remember is that it is not important if a story is completely exaggerated or plainly untrue. The most important thing about the story is in the telling. Storytelling harks back to an ancient time when the storytellers or *seanchaí* played an important role in the social life of the people as they gathered round the fire to hear a story being told.

Craic and *ceoil*

These are two words that sum up the Dubliner's attitude to life. *Craic* is an Irish word and it is really untranslatable. The closest you could get in English is probably 'fun' or 'having a laugh'. But *craic* is more than that. 'A bit of craic' can simply mean a bit of harmless teasing or slagging (as the locals call it), settling down in one of Dublin's famed hostelries for an evening of lively conversation and a few pints, perhaps a party, the enjoyment of a sporting event or a concert, or even just listening to a little music. This leads us to the second word *ceoil*, which is the Irish word for music. Dubliners love music no matter what the variety and will use any excuse to listen to some. *Ceoil* usually refers to traditional Irish music and there is no doubt that when there is *ceoil* there is definitely *craic* to be had as well.

Major festivals

The two major festivals celebrated in Dublin are the **St Patrick's Day** festival, held on 17 March, and **Christmas**.

Christmas is undoubtedly one of the most exciting times to visit Dublin. The atmosphere can be electric, especially the few days before Christmas Day as the city population swells to many times its normal size. Many of those Irish-born emigrants return to their families for Christmas. The pubs are full of old friends meeting for a catch-up drink. Grafton St fills up with buskers of all shapes and sizes from carol-singing choir groups to rock bands hoping to be spotted by a record company employee doing last-minute Christmas shopping. Moore St and Henry St, on the Northside of the Liffey, are thronged with traders selling cheap Christmas presents, decorations and wrapping paper. The place positively buzzes with energy.

Halloween (31 October) is also celebrated with fireworks, bonfires and the Samhain parade. Samhain was the ancient Irish harvest festival and many people dress up in scary costumes. Dracula is always a popular choice because the creator of the character, novelist Bram Stoker, was a Dubliner. There are traditionally fireworks on **New Year's Eve** over the Liffey to mark the beginning of a new year.

(*See pp22–3 for St Patrick's Day festival.*)

Culture and festivals

Craic and *ceoil* in a Dublin pub

St Patrick's Day

Every year on 17 March the whole world becomes Irish for a day to celebrate the feast of St Patrick, the patron saint of Ireland. Over 1 million people, in fair or foul weather, line the streets of Dublin to see the massive street parade that has now evolved into a carnival. In the past, the parade was a rather sombre affair with sponsored floats used merely by multinationals for advertising purposes. But since the mid-1990s it has become one big party and street theatre extravaganza. Theatre groups from all over the world are invited to perform.

Much of St Patrick's life is clouded in legend, and scholars for centuries have tried to discern what is true and what is false about his life. There are two manuscripts alleged to be the work of St Patrick, but they date from the 8th century and were copied by monks who, it seems, were also interested in raising the profile of the great saint for their own political ends. The myth of St Patrick is a good story and most Irish people will defend it vehemently even though some of the facts may seem a little surreal.

The myths of St Patrick

It is doubtful that St Patrick was the first Christian in Ireland or that he introduced Christianity to the whole country on his own. This was probably a myth propagated by the Irish Church in the 11th century. It is far more likely that there were already some Christians here, especially around the Dublin area and in the southeast of the country. The Irish raided the coasts of Britain and France during these times and took many slaves back to Ireland. It is probable that the first

Music is integral to the St Patrick's Day parade

An elaborate float at the parade

Christians were among these slaves and they may have converted some of the local population to their religion. St Patrick himself is said to have been brought as a slave to Ireland for the first time from somewhere near Carlisle in AD 432, but there was possibly a bishop named Palladius in the country before then.

Another myth associated with St Patrick is that he banished snakes from Ireland. However, there is evidence that before Patrick arrived there were no snakes, nor indeed any reptiles in the country. There are doubts that he even visited one of his famous pilgrimage sites, Lough Derg in Donegal, and even that he visited Dublin at all. Two places, Antrim and Downpatrick in the North of Ireland, claim to be St Patrick's last resting place.

Yet whatever the truth about St Patrick's life, you would do well to keep quiet about any doubts you may have about the saint. Dubliners will defend their patron saint with great passion.

Impressions

The centre of Dublin is quite compact and you can walk quite comfortably around it to see the major sights. There are many small cobbled streets with little traffic and there are plans to make the city more pedestrian-friendly. It has come a long way since the Vikings founded a settlement here in the 9th century. Dublin is now a bustling cosmopolitan city in a state of flux, with redevelopments and urban regeneration schemes constantly on the go.

Layout of the city

There are two well-defined areas to the centre of the city, divided by the River Liffey that flows from west to east through it – the Northside and the Southside. The main axis that runs through the city is the thoroughfare of O'Connell St on the Northside and the pedestrianised Grafton St on the Southside. The Southside is generally seen as more affluent, with the more exclusive boutiques and shopping arcades around the Grafton St area. For the last 15 years the city has been undergoing a transformation. In the 1990s the Temple Bar cultural area on the Southside was developed with a great degree of success. Traditionally the Northside has been neglected, but three major redevelopment projects are under way here.

When to go

There is no good or bad time to go to Dublin. The weather is usually better in the summer months and there is much more to do and see, but there are more tourists around. Christmas in Dublin or spending St Patrick's festival in the city can make for a special experience, but there will be many tourists about and hotel beds can be at a premium. Theoretically, the worst months to go to Dublin are November, January and February, but if you visit when the Rugby Internationals in the Six Nations Championship are on, you could have the time of your life.

Getting around

The best way to get around Dublin is on foot. It is a compact city and by walking you can get a real flavour of the city. Taxis are slightly more plentiful than they used to be, but they are expensive and it can be difficult to procure one on the street late on a weekend evening.

Dublin Bus offers an extensive service; you can go practically anywhere in the city on a bus or at least get within walking distance of where you want to go.

Dublin Bikes (*www.dublinbikes.ie*) is newly arrived in the city. For the cost of a three-day pass you can take one of the clunky-looking bikes from its stand and use it to get around the centre or go even further. Locks are provided, or you can leave the bike at another stand and pick up another one next time you need it. However, often the service seems erratic and it can be slow depending on the traffic. At rush hour a bus can be a better option than driving yourself because the buses use special lanes.

Dublin Area Rapid Transport (DART) is an excellent electric train service, but it only runs the length of Dublin Bay. If you are staying in the southern or northern suburbs on the coast, the DART is a great option for getting into the city. The Luas (Irish for 'speed') tram connects Sandyford to St Stephen's Green (Green Line) and Tallaght to Connolly (Red Line) and is a useful way of getting around the centre if you don't want to walk far. Plans are under way for a considerable extension to the Luas system, and by 2011 the red line will branch from Connolly station into the docklands area, while both the outer parts of the red and green lines will extend further to Saggart and Cherrywood, respectively.

Driving in the city

Just like any other major city, driving is difficult in central Dublin and traffic congestion is one of the most troublesome things about visiting the city. If you have your own car, you can drive into the city centre, although finding a parking space can be stressful. If you can avoid driving in the city centre, do so because you will enjoy your stay more. The times to avoid driving into central Dublin are the rush hours during the week. These stretch from about 8am until 9.30am and from about 5pm until 6.30pm. Driving out of the city during the morning rush hour or driving into the city during the evening rush hour is usually not too bad. Driving during the weekends is usually straightforward. The worst times for traffic jams are the Friday evening rush hour while it is raining, especially in winter if it is dark as well.

Reflected fireworks over the Liffey

Parking in the city

The only disadvantage of waiting until the end of the early-morning rush hour is that all of the parking spaces will have gone. It is fairly easy to get short-term parking spots for an hour or two in the centre of the city, particularly around the St Stephen's Green or Merrion Square area, but sometimes even these are scarce. Your best option for long-term parking is to go to one of the city-centre car parks.

Parking at the weekend or in the evenings after rush hour is much easier.

You pay for parking by feeding a parking meter with coins or by buying a parking disc from the nearest newsagent to where you want to park. Do not try to avoid paying and do not park illegally because your vehicle will be clamped and towed away. After a certain time in the evening, usually 7pm, parking is free in the centre of the city. Parking is also free on Sundays.

Pollution and littering

Littering remains a significant problem in the city, despite the fines threatened by the city council. The River Liffey is not as polluted as it used to be 20 years ago, but the increased traffic in the city has now made exhaust fumes the biggest pollutant for the city, exacerbated in the rush hour.

Manners and mores

If you meet someone for the first time, it is normal for an Irish person to shake your hand. Irish people also gesticulate a lot when they are speaking. If you turned down the volume of their voices, you might think the Irish to be from Southern Europe.

Generally Dublin is a relaxed city and you do not need to be very formal. If you go to dine in the top restaurants, however, men will have to wear a suit or jacket and tie, depending on the particular establishment. People are usually friendly and helpful in the streets, and if you need any help you just need to ask.

Swearing is not a social stigma and you should not be offended no matter what word a Dubliner, male or female, uses if they are smiling and using a friendly tone. In Ireland, swear words are part of the language and are how people express their emotions. Dubliners are an emotive lot. It is by the tone and the force of how the word is used that you can measure the seriousness of the words coming out. Do be careful if you go native with the language you use, though; not everyone is happy about the use of swear words and elderly people in particular may be offended. Some of the words are inoffensive derivatives of more serious words that have been invented by those literary Irish.

The cost of living

Dublin has a reputation for being an expensive place to visit. Eating out in restaurants can be particularly pricey.

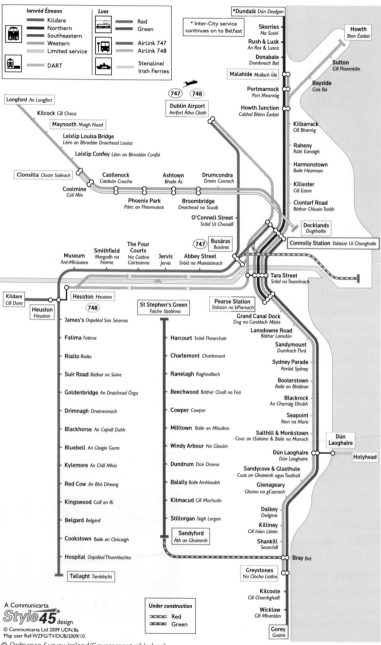

Iarnród Éireann
- Kildare
- Northern
- Southeastern
- Western
- Limited service
- DART

Luas
- Red
- Green
- Airlink 747
- Airlink 748
- Stenaline/Irish Ferries

*Dundalk *Dún Dealgan*

* Inter-City service continues on to Belfast

Skerries *Na Sceirí*
Rush & Lusk *An Ros & Lusca*
Donabate *Domhnach Bat*
Malahide *Mullach Íde*
Portmarnock *Port Mearnóg*
Howth Junction *Cabhal Bhinn Éadair*

Howth *Binn Éadair*
Sutton *Cill Fhionntáin*
Bayside *Cois Bá*

Kilbarrack *Cill Bharróg*
Raheny *Ráth Eanaigh*
Harmonstown *Baile Hearman*
Killester *Cill Easra*
Clontarf Road *Bóthar Chluain Tarbh*

Longford *An Longfort*
Kilcock *Cill Choca*
Maynooth *Maigh Nuad*
Leixlip Louisa Bridge *Léim an Bhradáin Droichead Louisa*
Leixlip Confey *Léim an Bhradáin Confaí*
Clonsilla *Cluain Saileach*
Coolmine *Cúil Mín*
Castleknock *Caisleán Cnucha*
Ashtown *Bhaile Ás*
Drumcondra *Droim Conrach*
Phoenix Park *Páirc an Fhionnuisce*
Broombridge *Droichead na Scuab*

O'Connell Street *Sráid Uí Chonaill*

Docklands *Dugthaithe*
Connolly Station *Stáisiún Uí Chonghaile*

747 748
Dublin Airport *Aerfort Átha Cliath*

Museum *Ard-Mhúsaem*
Smithfield *Margadh na Feirme*
The Four Courts *Na Ceithre Cúirteanna*
Jervis *Jervis*
Abbey Street *Sráid na Mainistreach*
747 Busáras *Busáras*

Tara Street *Sráid na Teamhrach*

Kildare *Cill Dara*
Heuston *Heuston*
748
Heuston *Heuston*

St Stephen's Green *Faiche Stiabhna*

Pearse Station *Stáisiún na bPiarsach*
Grand Canal Dock *Dug na Canálach Móire*
Lansdowne Road *Bóthar Lansdún*
Sandymount *Dumhach Thrá*
Sydney Parade *Paráid Sydney*
Booterstown *Baile an Bhóthair*
Blackrock *An Charraig Dhubh*
Seapoint *Rinn na Mara*
Salthill & Monkstown *Cnoc an tSalainn & Baile na Manach*

James's *Ospidéal San Séamas*
Fatima *Fatima*
Rialto *Rialto*
Suir Road *Bóthar na Siúire*
Goldenbridge *An Droichead Órga*
Drimnagh *Droimeanach*
Blackhorse *An Capall Dubh*
Bluebell *An Cloigín Gorm*
Kylemore *An Chill Mhór*
Red Cow *An Bó Dhearg*
Kingswood *Coill an Rí*
Belgard *Belgard*
Cookstown *Baile an Chócaigh*
Hospital *Ospidéal Thamhlachta*
Tallaght *Tamhlacht*

Harcourt *Sráid Fhearchair*
Charlemont *Charlemont*
Ranelagh *Raghnallach*
Beechwood *Bóthar Choill na Feá*
Cowper *Cowper*
Milltown *Baile an Mhuilinn*
Windy Arbour *Na Glasáin*
Dundrum *Dún Droma*
Balally *Baile Amhlaoibh*
Kilmacud *Cill Mochuda*
Stillorgan *Stigh Lorgan*
Sandyford *Áth an Ghainimh*

Dún Laoghaire *Dún Laoghaire*
Holyhead

Sandycove & Glasthule *Cuas an Ghainimh agus Tuathail*
Glenageary *Gleann na gCaorach*
Dalkey *Deilginis*
Killiney *Cill Iníon Léinín*
Shankill *Seanchill*
Bray *Bré*

Greystones *Na Clocha Liatha*
Kilcoole *Cill Chomhghaill*
Wicklow *Cill Mhantáin*
Gorey *Guaire*

A Communicarta
Style 45 design
© Communicarta Ltd 2009 UDN.8a
Map user Ref:WZFG/TV/DUB/2009/I0

Under construction
- Red
- Green

© Ordnance Survey Ireland/Government of Ireland

Architecture

Most of the oldest Dublin architecture is Georgian and it was a great city in those times, second only to London in the British Empire. Few of the buildings from medieval times remain and most have been renovated or have undergone major transformations from their original structure. Construction is currently underway of radical new developments that will transform the face of the city.

Medieval remnants of Old Dublin

The oldest buildings in Dublin cluster around the site of the original settlement. The great cathedrals of **Christchurch** and **St Patrick's** underwent extensive renovation in Victorian times. **Dublin Castle** is very different from what it must have been like in the Middle Ages.

The old city walls do remain in some places, but most are underground except for a section of the old medieval city gate below St Audoen's Church (St Audoen's Gate) and at Cornmarket. During the controversial building of the Dublin Corporation Offices over the ancient site at Wood Quay, some sections of the wall were uncovered, but they were destroyed during construction.

Georgian architecture

The greatest architectural treasures that Dublin possesses are of Georgian origin, and we take a stroll around some of the famous Georgian squares

of Dublin (*see pp32–3*). The 18th century was a period of great confidence in Dublin. During this time many of the great civic buildings like the **Customs House**, the **Four Courts** and the graceful Georgian squares and streets of the city were constructed.

The Wide Streets Commissioners, a body which received a grant for civic

Four Courts reflected in the Liffey

Customs House: the grandest Georgian building of them all

improvements from the Irish Parliament, were influential in this. They also laid down guidelines for property speculators regarding façade treatment and architectural elements. After the Act of Union of 1800, which led to the Dissolution of Grattan's Parliament, as it was known, the Wide Streets Commissioners began to lose their influence.

There was little enthusiasm for financing civic improvements in Dublin at the Parliament in London, especially as many of Dublin's buildings and streets were finer than those of the English capital.

Victorian Dublin

During the Victorian era Dublin went into decline and there was not much construction of new buildings. After Catholic Emancipation in 1829 many new Catholic churches, such as St Audoen's, were built in the city, generally to a classic Victorian design. Many of the old Dublin pubs are Victorian in design. The Stag's Head in Dame Court is a good example. In the 1840s (the time of the Great Famine), and with the increased poverty in the city, the great Georgian mansions fell into disrepair and became tenements.

Modern developments

There are not many architecturally significant modern buildings in Dublin, but this is set to change with ambitious redevelopment plans already afoot.

Busáras on Store St (Dublin central bus station) is a building for architecture buffs. It was the first truly modern building in the city. If you are not a real aficionado of buildings you might ask what the fuss is about, but architects from around the world rave about this structure. It was one of the original buildings inspired by the International Modernism school of architecture and was influenced by the work of Le Corbusier.

The rather dilapidated-looking **Liberty Hall** is currently the only skyscraper in Dublin because there was a height restriction imposed by the city (which has now just been lifted).

To mark the millennium, a huge face-lift of the inner city began, with O'Connell St, the crumbling docks and old Smithfield as its focus. The docklands have become a little concrete parkland with lots of open spaces, weekend markets, and shiny new glass and steel buildings. O'Connell St got its spire (or the 'stiletto in the ghetto' as local wags quickly named it), several old buildings were flattened, and there's hope that the credit crunch won't stop its long-deserved

Liberty Hall, Dublin's only skyscraper

DUBLIN'S BRIDGES

The bridges over the Liffey are important landmarks in the city centre. The **Ha'penny Bridge** is the most famous. It was constructed in 1816 from cast iron and, for the first year, an old halfpenny was charged as a toll.

The bridge closest to the sea is the **East Link Bridge** (1984), which is a toll bridge. The oldest bridge is the **Queen Maeve**, built in 1764, although the **Father Mathew Bridge** is on the site of the ancient Ford of Hurdles. The **Millennium Bridge** (1999) is a simple-span pedestrian bridge. **Grattan Bridge** (1874) is an ornate green bridge with iron lampstands that have horse decorations at their base. The modernistic **Sean O'Casey Pedestrian Bridge** (2005) links the two sides of the docklands project, while further downstream the strange new harp-shaped **Samuel Becket Bridge** (2010) will carry traffic and can be raised to allow shipping through. It will connect Guild Street and Sir John Rogerson's Quay.

regeneration. Smithfield, too, blossoms with plazas, high-rent apartments and offices, and some of the older buildings have been attractively accommodated rather than razed. In the docks area, strikingly designed bridges link the two sides of the river, and a stunning new conference centre and a new theatre grace the riverscape. North of the city, new architectural wonders include Terminal Two at Dublin airport. Whether it all continues, and we will see the proposed U2 tower in the docklands, and the gaps in O'Connell St turn into beautiful new offices and shops, is anyone's guess.

The International Financial Services Centre, Docklands

Walk: Georgian Dublin

A stroll around Georgian Dublin is as pleasant a tour as you can make of the city. For the purpose of this walk we start at Connolly DART and Rail station, but you can omit some of the walk and start on the Southside if you feel like a more leisurely amble.

Allow 2 hours for the whole route.

From Connolly Station walk north. At the junction of Amiens St and Killarney St, turn left. Look out for the Georgian Five Lamps with the lion motif on the base.

Turn right at Gardiner St and walk up to Mountjoy Square.

1 Mountjoy Square

Legend has it that Brian Boru, High King of Ireland, pitched his tent on the site of Mountjoy Square when he won the Battle of Clontarf in 1014. Playwright Sean O'Casey lived here.
Walk around the square to your right and down Great Denmark St past Belvedere House, to Parnell Square.

2 Parnell Square

Parnell Square is home of Charlemont House, which houses The Hugh Lane Gallery and also the Dublin Writers' Museum.
Walk around Parnell Square and then along O'Connell St to cross O'Connell Bridge into Westmoreland St.

3 Bank of Ireland building

This was the first purpose-built Parliament House in the world. The original House of Lords remains intact. *Entry is via Westmoreland St.*

4 Trinity façade

The main gate of Trinity College is a stone façade built in the 1750s. A popular meeting place for Dubliners. *Walk around the railings of Trinity to your left and along Grafton Street to St Stephen's Green.*

5 St Stephen's Green

There are three elegant buildings in a row here. Two of Dublin's finest Georgian buildings are Newman House and Iveagh House. The third is University Church, which has a lavish interior.
Exit St Stephen's Green via Leeson St and turn left onto Pembroke St. Fitzwilliam Square will be on your right as you walk down the street. Walk around the square then left along Fitzwilliam Place to Fitzwilliam St.

6 and 7 Fitzwilliam Square and No 29 Fitzwilliam St

The Fitzwilliam family, Earls of Merrion, developed the area as part of their estate in the late 18th century. No 29 Fitzwilliam St is a restored Georgian house run by the Electricity Supply Board (ESB) and the National Museum of Ireland. It is now a visitor centre and here you can see how a middle-class Georgian family lived.

Merrion Square is to your left as you approach the end of Fitzwilliam St.

8 Merrion Square

Merrion Square is one of the largest, and probably the finest, of Dublin's Georgian squares.

Walk around the square into the west side.

9 Leinster House

Originally erected during the great Georgian building spree by Richard Cassells for Lord Kildare, this building was created with two fronts. It is currently home to the Irish Dáil.

Walk: Georgian Dublin

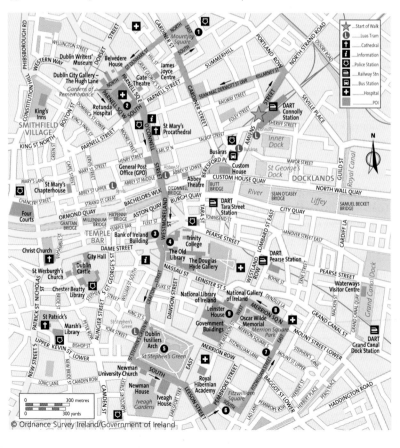

© Ordnance Survey Ireland/Government of Ireland

Breweries and distilleries

There is no question that Ireland is famous for its alcohol, and two of its finest exports are produced in Dublin: the world-famous Guinness® stout and Jameson's whiskey. In Ireland whiskey is spelt with an 'e' and there is much friendly rivalry between the Scots and the Irish about who created whiskey first.

Guinness® Storehouse

The black stuff is the favoured drink of the true Dubliner. There is no better pint, and for many visitors to Dublin a visit to the home of Guinness® at St James's Gate is like a pilgrimage. Arthur Guinness founded the Guinness® brewery in 1759 when he leased the premises for £45 per annum. A visit to the Guinness® Storehouse, which houses the **World of Guinness® Exhibition** and displays some of those famous ads, will educate you about Dublin's most famous drink.

About 10 million glasses of Guinness® are drunk every day (a bit more on St Patrick's Day!) and Guinness® is sold in over 150 countries.

Although there are rumours that there is a secret ingredient to Guinness® (and there may well be one kept secret by the brewers), the basic ingredients are quite simple and all natural: roasted and malted barley, hops, yeast and water. The yeast is grown from the original strain which was used by Arthur Guinness all those years ago. The water is not actually from the Liffey as some locals might lead you to believe. It is from a freshwater spring in the Wicklow Mountains. Although Guinness® is called black, it is in fact a dark ruby colour; you will see this if you hold your pint up to the light.

Guinness® is good for you

It may seem strange to some, but the advertising of Guinness®' health benefits is partially to blame for the success of the brewery. Stout is full of iron and the vitamin B12 and was recommended to pregnant women to prevent them from becoming anaemic. The alcohol content of Guinness® is lower than some other beers at 4.2 per cent alcohol by volume.

The perfect pint

Guinness® does not travel very well and if you want to drink the best pint of Guinness® you have ever had, you need to drink it in Dublin. Although it is also brewed abroad, it never tastes quite as good. The perfect pint should taste smooth and creamy. The most important people are the bartenders, who should keep the pipes used to transport the Guinness® from the keg to the tap in pristine condition. The next factor is their pint-pulling skills – they must use the 'two part pour'. The pint is started by filling a clean and dry glass to three-quarters full with the glass held at a 45° angle to the tap. Then the pint is left to settle properly. It is then filled to the top and it should have a creamy head, produced by nitrogen gas.

The importance of a good pint of Guinness® cannot be overestimated and some experienced stout drinkers are very fussy about what watering hole they drink in and who pulls their pints. There has been considerable heated debate among regular stout drinkers through the years as to which is the best pub for Guinness®. You are better off trying a few and deciding for yourself which is your own personal favourite drinking establishment.

Breweries and distilleries

Black magic

The Gravity Bar is a good place to try your first pint, and you can get a commanding view of the city from here on a clear day.

The Gravity Bar, top floor, Guinness® Storehouse, St James's Gate. Tel: (01) 408 4800. www.guinness-storehouse.com. Open: Sept–Jun 9.30am–5pm; Jul–Aug 9.30am–9pm (last admission 7pm). Admission charge. A 20-minute walk from city centre.

Bus: 51B, 78A, 123. Luas: James's.

Old Jameson Distillery

This is no longer a distillery but an interactive visitor centre that provides an introduction to the distillation of the 'hard stuff', as the locals call whiskey. Jameson's produced the world-famous brand here until it was taken over by the Irish Distillers Group, and now its production has been moved to a brand-new state-of-the-art distillery in Middleton, County Cork. After a visit you will be able to distinguish between the smoother and more refined triple-distilled malts produced by the Irish and the smokier and peatier whiskies produced by the Scots. After a trip around the distillery your head will be spinning with information about the scientific technology required for distillation. Luckily, they give you a wee drop of the water of life, as it is called in Irish (*uisge beatha*), to settle you back down.

Old Jameson Distillery, Bow St. Tel: (01) 807 2355. www.jamesonwhiskey.com. Open: 9am–6.30pm. Last tour 5.30pm. Visits by guided tour only. Admission charge. Bus: 68, 69, 79 from Aston Quay; 90 from Connolly/Heuston Stations. Luas: Smithfield.

HOW TO DRINK WHISKEY

There are myriad ways of drinking whiskey. To get the true flavour of one of Ireland's top malts you really should drink it neat or at least only with ice or diluted a little with tap water. Drinking it with 'nothing in it' is often touted by serious aficionados as the only way to drink whiskey; others will say that it should only be consumed with a drop of water to get the true flavour. But it is really unnecessarily snobbish to suggest that whiskey should only be drunk in one way as it really is a matter of personal taste as to how you like to take your whiskey. Some whiskey brands blend really well with mixers and are complemented by a whole range of flavours. Many of the trendy young locals will invent their own mixer in which to douse their whiskey and the manufacturers for one don't mind. Most Dubliners who mix their whiskey most commonly mix it with cola. In the winter one of the most common ways to drink whiskey is in the form of a hot toddy. This is a delicious and very practical way to stave off the cold winter chill. The whiskey is served in a glass with hot water, a slice of lemon, cloves and sugar. On particularly cold days the bar staff will have the kettle on the boil continuously; it is one of the most pleasant ways to get merry. At Christmas Irish coffees are a tradition, but in most bars, hotels and restaurants you can get them at any time of the year. Made with coffee, sugar and cream, they are weight-gain-inducing fare. This is one of the most luxuriant drinks invented, and if you have one in the middle of the day don't plan to do anything strenuous in the afternoon – go for a snooze back at the hotel instead.

Interior of the Old Jameson Distillery

Dublin's canals, docks and quays

The Grand Canal and the Royal Canal were both built to connect Dublin to the River Shannon in the West of Ireland and form a loop around the centre of the city. The docks are the sites of the greatest urban regeneration in the city.

The Grand Canal

This is the older of the two Dublin canals and it was built between 1756 and 1803, but has not been in commercial use since the 1960s. The walk along the canal was immortalised in verse by poet Patrick Kavanagh: 'Leafy with love banks and the green waters of the canal'. The Monaghan-born poet lived in Dublin and gleaned much inspiration from walking along the canalside.

One of the most pleasant areas of the canal and a perfect place for a morning stroll is the stretch from Mount St Bridge to Leeson St Bridge. If you walk on the Northside you will pass by the bronze statue of the great Mr Kavanagh himself reclining on a seat, perhaps as he did in the 1940s and 1950s.

Waterways Visitor Centre

An exhibition about Ireland's inland waterways and canals housed in a modern building in Grand Canal Basin. *Grand Canal Quay.*
Tel: (01) 677 7510. Open: Jun–Sept 9.30am–5.30pm; Oct–May Wed–Sun 12.30–5pm.

The Royal Canal

Built in 1790 by Long John Binns, this was intended to be a competitor to the Grand Canal. Binns was a former employee of the Grand Canal Company. The Duke of Leinster provided money for the construction of the canal provided that it passed by his mansion in Maynooth. The canal now sits disused and there are railway tracks alongside some of its length from a railway company that bought it in the 1840s. The Royal Canal towpath is a pleasant place to walk, particularly if you walk near the Binns Bridge in Drumcondra. The Blessington St Basin was used as a filter bed when water from the Royal Canal was being put in the city's drinking water supply. Now it makes for an agreeable park area.
Short walk from O'Connell St at the end of Blessington St. Open during daylight hours. Free admission. Bus: 10.

Docks and Quays

The long decline in the Dublin Docks has led to their being the focus of the regeneration of the city in the last decade. The Docklands is centred around St George's Dock, which is where a lot of the urban regeneration has taken place. Grand Canal Dock is the site of a new DART station and the Waterways Visitor Centre.

The quays are the streets that run parallel to the Liffey. As the city undergoes its regeneration the riverside will play an increasing role in the social fabric of the city. The development of the Liffey Boardwalk and the new bridges have instigated that process.

Barges are still used on the Grand Canal

Churches and cathedrals

The major churches and cathedrals in Dublin are Protestant and there are few Catholic churches of medieval origin. The two great Norman cathedrals, Christ Church and St Patrick's, are the major attraction. In times past, the Protestant church was the major landowner in Dublin, with the city carved up between Christ Church and St Patrick's Cathedrals, but this is no longer the case. Most of the existing churches are a mixture of architectural styles.

Christ Church Cathedral

Christ Church dates from about 1038 when Viking King Sitric (the first Christian Norse king) constructed a cathedral on the site. However, this original building is long gone as it was only made of wood. The present building was founded in about 1172 by Richard de Clare (Strongbow), the Norman knight and overlord, and Archbishop Laurence O'Toole, who later became the city's patron saint. After many different restorations, the building now looks more Victorian than anything else. The cathedral crosses Winetavern St by a covered bridge to the **Synod Hall**, home of the Dublinia Experience. The oldest part of the cathedral is the crypt, dating from 1188, and one of the largest medieval crypts still intact. The **Treasures of Christchurch** exhibition displays manuscripts, historical artefacts and some fascinating gold and silverware. The display includes a silver plate donated by William of Orange in thanksgiving for his victory at the Battle of the Boyne in 1690. The choir is a descendant, with the St Patrick's cathedral choir, of the choir that sang the premiere of Handel's *Messiah*. The choir sings at Sunday and weekday Anglican services. Strongbow's tomb is in the cathedral, and the medieval reliquary is said to contain the heart of St Laurence. During the year there is a series of events held in Christ Church including recitals and concerts. It is worth calling ahead to see if anything is on during your stay. Choral services are held on Tuesday, Wednesday and Thursday at 6pm, on Saturday at 5pm, and on Sunday at 11am and 3.30pm. *Christchurch Place. Tel: (01) 677 8099. Fax: (01) 677 8099. www.cccdub.ie. Open: Sept–May Mon–Sat 9.45am–4.15pm, Sun 12.30–2.30pm; Jun–mid-Jul Mon, Tue & Fri 9.45am–6.15pm, Wed, Thur & Sat 9.45am–4.15pm, Sun 12.30–2.30pm & 4.30–6.15pm; mid-Jul–Aug Mon–Fri 9.45am–6.15pm, Sat 9.45am–4.15pm, Sun 12.30–2.30pm & 4.30–6.15pm. Admission charge which includes entry to*

Treasures of Christchurch exhibition. It is about a 15-minute walk up Dame St and Lord Edward St from the main entrance gate to Trinity College. Bus: 78A from Aston Quay, 50 from Eden Quay.

Newman University Church

A favourite with locals for weddings because of its glitzy interior, this tiny church snuggled in between two Georgian houses in St Stephen's Green is well worth a visit. Commissioned by Cardinal Newman in the nineteenth century, it is in the Byzantine style, covered in green marble and polychromatic brickwork, and has an unusual belltower.

7A St Stephen's Green South. Tel: (01) 478 1606. Open: Mon–Fri 9am–5pm, Sat 9am–5.30pm, Sun 9am–4pm. Free admission.

St Audoen's Churches

There are two churches side by side called St Audoen's; the Protestant church is the older of the two. The church is named after St Ouen, the patron saint of Normandy and archbishop of Rouen. The bells in the 12th-century tower are among the oldest church bells still working in Ireland. St Audoen's is the only surviving medieval church in Dublin. The existing church was built here in 1190 to replace an earlier structure dedicated to St Colmcille. It is said to have three bells dating from 1423 hanging in the tower. In the main porch there is an early Christian gravestone known as the Lucky Stone, which has been kept here since before 1309 and has many strange legends connected with it. St Audoen's Catholic Church

Christ Church Cathedral

St Audoen's Protestant Church

was built much later, and has an impressive façade.

Cornmarket, High St. Tel: (01) 677 0088. Open: Jun–Sept daily 9.30am–4.45pm. Admission charge.

St Mary's Chapterhouse

All that remains of the once great St Mary's Benedictine Abbey is the Chapterhouse. There is an exhibition and a model of what the Abbey may have looked like in medieval times.

Meetinghouse Lane. Tel: (01) 872 1490. Open: mid-Jun–mid-Sept Wed & Sun 10am–5pm. Admission charge.

St Mary's Procathedral

St Mary's Procathedral is the Catholic cathedral, built between 1816 and 1825. It is a much more austere building than the two great Norman cathedrals. It is the home of the Palaestrina choir who sing at the 11am Mass every Sunday. This is probably the most talented choir in the country, and if you are in the centre of the city at this time you should definitely take the opportunity to attend one of the services.

83 Marlborough St. Tel: (01) 874 5441. www.procathedral.ie. Open: Mon–Fri 7.30am–6.45pm, Sat 7.30am–7.15pm, Sun 9am–1.45pm & 5–7.45pm. Free admission.

St Patrick's Cathedral

In 1191 John Comyn, Archbishop of Dublin, built the second great cathedral of Dublin. It might seem strange to have two cathedrals so close to each other in the city, but Comyn decided that Christ Church was too much under the control of the Viceroy and that the Church needed its own cathedral. St Patrick's Cathedral was established outside the city walls and was considered a Celtic cathedral because of the association with the patron saint. It was built on the grounds of an earlier church on the site that, since the late 5th century, legend has associated with Patrick himself. St Patrick is said to have baptised some converts in a well that used to be in the gardens beside the cathedral. A fire in 1362 destroyed some of the building. Jonathan Swift, author of *Gulliver's Travels*, was Dean of the cathedral for many years.

St Patrick's Close. Tel: (01) 453 9472. www.stpatrickscathedral.ie. Open: Nov–Feb 9am–5pm, only open until 3pm on Sat & Sun. Admission charge.

St Werburgh's Church

This church is named after the Abbess of Ely who died around AD 700. The church was damaged by fire in 1754, leaving only the tower and façade intact. St Werburgh's once boasted a fine tower and spire. However, it was removed in late 1836 as it was feared it might be used during a rebellion as a sniper position.

Werburgh St. Tel: (01) 478 3710. Open: Mon–Fri 10am–4pm. Donation requested.

Whitefriar Street Carmelite Church

Although this church doesn't have a stunning medieval history or any over-the-top Victorian flying buttresses, it does have one or two claims to fame. One of them, set amidst the shrines to various other saints, is a reliquary containing the bones of St Valentine, brought back from Rome by Father John Spratt in the last century. He was given them by Pope Gregory XVI. They may not be the entire collection, however, since several churches in the UK also claim to be the protectors of St Valentine's remains. Also in the church, thanks to the same Father Spratt, is a 16th-century wooden carving of the Madonna, found in a junk shop and thought to have been used for some time as a pig trough. The church also has a little café.

56 Aungier St. Tel: (01) 475 8821. www.carmelites.ie. Open: daily.

Dublin Castle and City Hall

The seat and epicentre of imperialist British rule for seven centuries produces ambivalent feelings among Dubliners, especially the older generation. Dubliners note with irony that even the great statue of the Figures of Justice turns its back on the city inhabitants just like the harsh foreign rulers did.

Dublin Castle

Dublin Castle is believed to be on the site of an ancient Gaelic ring fort and after that perhaps a Viking fortification of some sort. The Norman castle was founded in 1204 by the Order of King John to provide fortification against the marauding O'Byrne and O'Toole tribes

A snake sculpture guards Dublin's black pool

of Wicklow. It is thought the record tower may be the only structure that is original, but even this has been renovated. After a fire in the 17th century, the castle was redesigned to its present form with the lower and upper yards. The current structure is a mix of architectural styles.

Dublin Castle survived various insurrections and many attacks. Some of those freedom fighters that tried and failed included Silken Thomas Fitzgerald, Edward Bruce and Robert Emmet. In 1916 the rebels in the Easter Rising also failed to take the castle. To add insult to injury, during the Great Famine of the 1840s when people were dying of starvation in the streets, the Viceroy entertained guests, and the balls, receptions and dinners continued in the Castle. It was eventually handed over to the Irish Free State, and when Michael Collins was told he was seven minutes late by the commanding officer he uttered those memorable words. 'We have been waiting over seven hundred

View of Dublin Castle from the Dubh Linn Gardens

years, you can have the extra seven minutes.' For the visitor to Dublin Castle, there is a wealth of treasures to explore, but without doubt the highlight is the **State Apartments**, which were the residence of the British Viceroy. To see

ONE THAT GOT AWAY

The Irish Crown Jewels were stolen from the Bedford Tower of Dublin Castle in 1907. It happened the day before the British king and queen were due to make a visit. It is not sure how the thief got into one of the most heavily fortified places in the world at the time. The culprit has never been found and the jewels are still missing.

St Patrick's Hall with the banners of the Knights of St Patrick and the frescoed ceiling depicting the history of Ireland is definitely worth the admission fee. The State Apartments are used for the inauguration of the President of Ireland, important state functions and official entertainment. They are sometimes used for heads of state and other visiting dignitaries and VIPs.

Cork Hill, Dame St. Tel: (01) 645 8813. www.dublincastle.ie.
Open: Mon–Fri 10am–4.45pm, Sat, Sun & Public Holidays 2–4.45pm. Admission charge.
Bus: 49, 56A, 77, 77A, 123.

The statue of justice at Dublin Castle

behind the castle grounds and in front of the Chester Beatty Library are the Dubh Linn Gardens (*see p48 & p50*).

Chester Beatty Library

Housed in the European Museum of the Year 2002, this is one of those must-see sights, and it is one of Dublin's greatest treasures. Sir Alfred Chester Beatty was an American mining magnate and an art and manuscripts collector. He built up a fabulous collection in his lifetime, which he bequeathed to the Irish nation. In 1957 he became the first honorary Irish citizen because of this. The collection includes thousands of manuscripts, rare books and valuable artefacts from eastern Islamic cultures and from the Far East. The second floor, devoted to the religions of the world, has a whole range of religious texts and artefacts. Some of the highlights include hundreds of copies of the Islamic holy book, the Koran (including some very rare ones), ancient papyri from Egypt, scrolls and artwork from China, Japan and Tibet and fragments of each of the New Testament gospels dating from the second and third centuries.

The Clock Tower Building, Dublin Castle. Tel: (01) 407 0750. Email: info@cbl.ie. www.cbl.ie. Open: May–Sept Mon–Fri 10am–5pm, Sat 11am–5pm, Sun 1–5pm; Oct–Apr Tue–Fri 10am–5pm, Sat 11am–5pm, Sun 1–5pm. Free admission. Bus: 13, 16, 19, 50, 54A, 56A, 77, 77A, 78A, 123.

City Hall

The City Hall, one of the finest Georgian buildings in the city, was built between 1769 and 1779 by the Guild of Merchants and used as the Royal Exchange. It was built on the site of a nunnery called St Mary del Dame, from which this street derives its name. The circular entrance hall or rotunda has a mosaic of the city crest on the floor, an incredible domed ceiling and some impressive statues, including a huge one of the Liberator Daniel O'Connell.

There is a multimedia exhibition describing the history of Dublin called 'The Story of the Capital'. The exhibition traces the evolution of the capital through the ages from before the Anglo-Norman invasion of 1170 to the present day. In former times, City Hall was notorious as a site of repression; the rebels of 1798 were tortured here and public whippings were also performed.

It was taken over and used by Dublin Corporation in 1852 with proceedings taking a slightly less violent tone. The funeral of Charles Stewart Parnell was held here and the funeral procession of Michael Collins left from here. In 1995 Dublin Corporation moved to their new offices in Wood Quay, but Dublin city council still hold meetings here.

City Hall, Cork Hill, Dame St. Tel: (01) 222 2204. www.dublincity.ie. Open: Mon–Sat 10am–5.15pm, Sun & Public Holidays 2–5pm. Admission charge. Bus: 50, 54, 56A, 77, 77A, 123.

Dublin Castle and City Hall

Walk: historical Dublin

On this walk we stroll around the sites associated wit[h] medieval Dublin. Although most of the ancient building[s] have been replaced by later Georgian structures, there ar[e] still a few remnants of ancient Dublin.

Allow 1 hour.

1 City Hall (*see p47*)

City Hall, one of Dublin's impressive Georgian edifices, was built for £58,000, most of which was raised by public lotteries.
Walk into the grounds of Dublin Castle and keep left around the back of the castle. You will see a small garden on your left.

2 Dubh Linn Gardens

(*See p50 for details.*) *Walk through this garden, through the Castle gate and turn left on to Werburgh St.*

3 St Werburgh's Church

(*See p43 for details.*) *The street turns into Bride St. Keep walking until you reach Kevin St – turn right and then right again into St Patrick's Close.*

4 Marsh's Library

Archbishop Narcissus Marsh set up the first public library in Ireland. Sir William Robinson, who also designed the Royal Hospital at Kilmainham, designed the building. The interior of the library remains unchanged since it was built nearly 300 years ago. Readers were locked int[o] wire cages to ensure they did not steal the rare books.
St Patrick's Close. Tel: (01) 454 3511. Open: Mon, Wed & Fri 10am–1pm & 2–5pm, Sat 10.30am–1pm. Small admission charge.

5 St Patrick's Cathedral

The great Norman church of which writer Jonathan Swift was Dean for a while (*see p43*).
Turn right into Patrick St and walk up to Christchurch Place.

6 Christ Church Cathedral/ Dublinia

Strongbow, the conqueror of Dublin, built the other great Gothic Norman church of Dublin on top of an earlier Viking church (*see p40*). The Dublinia centre is in the Synod Hall.
Dublinia. Tel: (01) 679 4611.

*www.dublinia.ie. Open: Apr–Sept daily
10am–5pm; Oct–Mar Mon–Fri
11am–4pm, weekends & Public Holidays
10am–4pm. Admission charge.
Walk through the arch and down
towards the river. Turn left on to Cook St.*

7 St Audoen's Gate

The sole surviving city gate is visible
below St Audoen's Church on Cook St.
It was one of the main entrances into
the medieval city.

*Turn right on Bridge St towards
the river.*

8 Brazen Head Inn

Although the Brazen Head pub was
actually built in 1668, there is a local
belief that the building is on the site
of a long succession of pubs that
stretches back to 1198, making it
the oldest drinking establishment in
the city.
Cross the Liffey here.

9 Father Mathew Bridge

Thought to be the original site of the
Ford of Hurdles that gave Dublin its
name in Irish.
Continue straight on into Church St.

10 St Michan's Church

(*See p91 for details.*)
*Walk around the back of the Four
Courts, then return to the bank of
the Liffey. Cross the Liffey again to
Wood Quay.*

11 Wood Quay/Isolde's Tower

Wood Quay has been replaced by the
Dublin Corporation building called the
Bunker. This area is the oldest part of
the city, with Fishamble St being the
centre of the old Viking town. Isolde
Tower is opposite the pub with the same
name, and incorporated into a modern
block of apartments are the remains of
the fortification tower that was used to
protect Dublin from pirates in Norman
times. The legend of Isolde and Tristan
is associated with it.

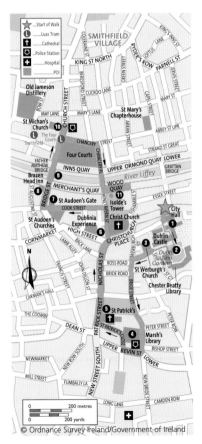

© Ordnance Survey Ireland/Government of Ireland

Gardens and parks

Although it may not seem like it at times, there is a considerable amount of greenery in Dublin. The parks and gardens of the city are an excellent place to have a picnic or go for a stroll to get away from the often frenetic activity in the streets. Phoenix Park is one of the largest parks in Europe and the home of Dublin Zoo.

Dubh Linn Gardens

In the grounds of Dublin Castle there is a small park with a fountain. This is what remains of the rather bigger black pool (Dubh Linn in Irish) that gave the city its name. The gardens are thought to be the location where the Liffey and the now underground River Poddle met at a much larger pool when the Vikings arrived to form their *longphort.*

Gardens of Remembrance

This small park in Parnell Square is a bit dilapidated, but it is worth a brief stop to take a look at the sculpture of *The Children of Lir* by sculptor Oísín Kelly, which depicts creatures from the mystical world of Celtic mythology.

Iveagh Gardens

The secret gardens of Dublin were once part of the walled grounds of Clonmel House and were owned by the Guinness family. In 1939 Lord Iveagh presented the gardens that bear his name to the government, who subsequently passed them on to the University College Dublin. The University was based in the building at that time, but now it has moved out to the Belfield Campus in the southern suburbs of the city. Part of the house is now the National Concert Hall. The gardens contain a maze, a grotto and a fountain.

You can access the Iveagh Gardens from Harcourt St or Earlsfort Terrace.

Merrion Square Park

This is a small park with elegant flowerbeds that blaze opulent colour in the spring. The highlight is the statue of Oscar Wilde.

Phoenix Park

Just west of the city centre, Phoenix Park is Dublin's largest patch of greenery.

In 1671 James Butler, Duke of Ormonde, developed Phoenix Park as a royal hunting park, and it was stocked with deer, pheasant and partridge. In

1745 Viceroy Lord Chesterfield opened the park to the public. It is the largest enclosed city-centre park in Europe and the Irish Government declared it a national historic park in 1986.

The park has always been associated with sporting events. Cricket and polo were the sports of the Anglo-Irish gentry and are still played today. In the 1920s Grand Prix races were held here. Now Gaelic football, hurling and soccer are played. Horseracing meetings are held at the Phoenix Park racecourse.

Phoenix Park is home to about 500 fallow deer that have been there since the early 17th century. If you want to see them up close it is best to go out early in the morning. For a walk around the park, *see pp52–3*.

St Stephen's Green

This park used to be an open tract of land for animal grazing; it was in fact an ancient commons (those granted the Freedom of the City still – technically – have the right to graze their sheep here!). In 1664 it was enclosed and an entrance fee was charged to enter. Then, in the late 17th century, it was converted into a city park. It was named after a hospital that catered for those suffering from leprosy. Sir Arthur Guinness, the fellow responsible for the black stuff, paid for the transformation.

The Fusilier's Arch, modelled on the Arch of Titus in Rome, is at the corner of St Stephen's Green and Grafton St. It was erected in 1907 to commemorate the men of the Royal Dublin Fusiliers who fell during the Boer War. There are duck ponds here and it is a Dublin tradition to feed the ducks in St Stephen's Green. The fine old bandstand, where summer performances are often held, was built for the jubilee of Queen Victoria. St Stephen's Green is popular with office workers at lunchtime, and it is a nice idea to join them on a warm summer day for a picnic or to eat a takeaway sandwich from one of the nearby cafés. *St Stephen's Green is at the top of Grafton St.*

St Stephen's Green makes for a pleasant escape

Walk: Phoenix Park

Phoenix Park is Dublin's proudest patch of greenery. It is just outside the centre and is a great place to escape to at any time of the day. In the early morning you will be able to catch glimpses of the deer. Getting there: Bus: 25, 25A, 26, 51, 51B, 66, 66A, 67, 67A.

The walk starts at the Wellington Monument near Wellington Road. Allow 1–2 hours.

1 Wellington Monument

The memorial to Wellington, who was actually a Dubliner, is the tallest obelisk in Europe. Completed in 1861, it is 62.5m (205ft) tall and was intended to be taller, but funds were too scarce.
Turn left on Chesterfield Avenue. The zoo is to the right.

2 The Zoo

The Phoenix Park zoo is one of Dublin's most popular tourist attractions. It was designed by Decimus Burton in 1830 and opened with one exhibit – a wild boar. Now there are various different species of animal, of which many are endangered and undergoing breeding programmes.
A famous resident of the Dublin zoo was the MGM lion that introduced their productions with a roar.
Tel: (01) 474 8900. www.dublinzoo.ie. Open: Mar–Sept daily 9.30am–6pm; Oct daily 9.30am–5.30pm; Nov–Feb daily 9.30am–4.30pm. Admission charge. Continue along Chesterfield Avenue.

3 The President's House

The official residence of the President of Ireland, this building is more popularly known by its Irish name, Áras an Uachtaráin. It looks a little like the American White House. You are also passing the spot where the infamous Phoenix Park murders occurred: on 6 May 1882 a radical national group calling themselves 'The Invincibles' murdered Lord Cavendish, the Chief Secretary, and Thomas Burke, his undersecretary.
Áras an Uachtaráin. Tel: (01) 677 0095. www.gov.ie/aras. Tours: Sat 10.15am– 4pm. Free admission. The Phoenix Monument is at the crossroads.

4 Phoenix Monument

Lord Chesterfield erected this monument to the mythical bird when he opened the park to the public. The phoenix in the park's name did not in fact come from the myth but from the Anglicisation of the Irish name, Fionn uisce. This means 'bright stream' and refers to a stream that flowed nearby.

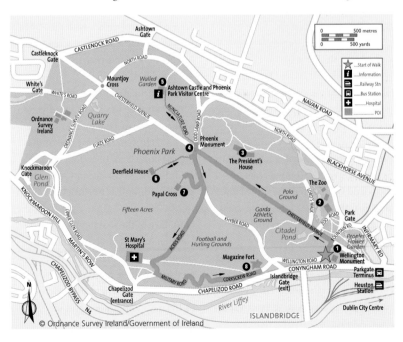

Turn right on to Odd Lamp Rd and left up to the visitor centre.

5 Ashtown Castle and Phoenix Park Visitor Centre

The gamekeepers who kept guard and made sure no Irish scoundrels stole any of the royal deer herd resided in Ashtown Castle, which is now a ruin. Next door the Visitor Centre provides information on the history of the park and its nature.

The Phoenix Park Visitor Centre. Tel: (01) 677 0095. Open: mid-Mar–Oct daily 10am–6pm; Nov–mid-Mar Wed–Sun 10am–5.30pm (closed: Mon & Tue). Free admission.
Retrace your steps, turn right, cross the Main Road and turn right.

6 Deerfield House

Once home to Lord Chesterfield, this is now the residence of the US Ambassador. *Go back to Khyber Road and turn right to reach Papal Cross.*

7 Papal Cross

This metal cross marks the spot where Pope John Paul II said Mass to over 1 million people in 1979.
Continue towards St Mary's Hospital, then left along Military Rd and Corkscrew Rd.

8 Magazine Fort

The fort was used to store British army munitions from 1735 until independence in 1922. In 1916 it was one of the targets of the rebels in the Easter Rising.

Walk: Phoenix Park

Glasnevin

The parish of Glasnevin, known in Celtic times as Glas Naeidhe, is located approximately 3km (2 miles) north of Dublin City. Glasnevin lies on fertile lowlands, fed by the rivers Tolka and Liffey. One of the river tributaries rises from the nearby Royal Canal. This suburb is the home of the Irish National Botanic Gardens and the largest cemetery in the whole of Ireland.

Glasnevin Cemetery

A trip to a graveyard may seem a macabre way to spend a morning, but the cemetery at Glasnevin is an education. It was opened in 1832 with the help of Daniel O'Connell just for Roman Catholics, and it was originally called Prospect Cemetery.

The huge central round tower was erected over the grave of the 'Liberator' when his body was moved here in 1847. Glasnevin Cemetery is the resting place of many of the most famous Irish people in history. Some of those buried here include Michael Collins, Charles Stewart Parnell, Sir Roger Casement, Jim Larkin, Eamonn DeValera, Countess Markievicz and Maud Gonne (the unrequited love of W B Yeats). Many of the gravestones are adorned with patriotic symbols, shamrocks and Celtic crosses.

Finglas Rd, Glasnevin. Tel: (01) 882 6500. www.glasnevin-cemetery.ie. Bus: 40 from Parnell St. Free admission. There are daily guided tours of the site at 2.30pm. Call to check. Admission charge for tour.

Parnell – the uncrowned king of Glasnevin Cemetery

Charles Stewart Parnell was the uncrowned King of Ireland. The charismatic orator was the leader of the Irish Home Rule Party and a leading campaigner for Home Rule. He was accused of involvement with the Phoenix Park murders in order to discredit him, but his affair with a married woman led to his political downfall.

He lost the backing of the Catholic Church, but he never lost the affection of the people of Dublin. He died aged only 45. His funeral drew one of the biggest crowds that Dublin ever saw. He is buried in Glasnevin Cemetery. On the monument to Parnell are the words, 'No man has the right to fix the boundary to the march of a nation. No man has a right to say to his country thus far shalt thou go and no further. We have never attempted to fix the *nec plus ultra* to the progress of Ireland's nationhood and we never shall.'

National Botanic Gardens

The National Botanic Gardens are the country's centre of botany and horticulture. The highlights of the gardens are the Georgian curvilinear greenhouses and the cast-iron palm house. Richard Turner, who designed the greenhouses in Kew Gardens in London, designed these and they were built from 1843 to 1869. On Addison's Walk some of the trees date from the 18th century.

Botanic Ave, Glasnevin. Tel: (01) 857 0909. www.botanicgardens.ie. Open: Nov–Feb 9am–4.30pm; Mar–Oct 9am–6pm. Closed: Christmas Day. Free admission. Bus: 4, 19 (O'Connell St); 13A (Merrion Sq).

An angel stands guard at O'Connell's Monument

Grafton St and the Southside

The Southside of Dublin is dominated by Grafton St, which is the most exclusive shopping street in the city, and the streets around the elegant Georgian squares and St Stephen's Green. It has a decidedly more affluent feel to it than the Northside, with many designer boutiques and exclusive shopping opportunities.

Bewley's Oriental Café

This Grafton St coffee shop is a favourite of Dublin shoppers. It has a fine and elegant Victorian interior.
78 Grafton St. Tel: (01) 672 7720.

Government Buildings

The impressive dome structure is a kind of mock Georgian design. It was the last British building and was built as a Royal College of Science. Organised tours of the building run on Saturdays when you can see the Taoiseach's office.
Upper Merrion St. Open: Sat 10.30am–2.15pm. Admission charge. Tickets for free tour available from the National Gallery. Admission by tour only.

Grafton St

Grafton St is the premier shopping street in Dublin. It is a completely pedestrianised street (since the 1980s), and there is a great atmosphere when the place is filled with chatting shoppers and talented buskers.

Leinster House

This is the house where the Irish Parliament, Dáil and the *Seanad* sit. Richard Castle designed the building for the Duke of Leinster and it was built in 1745.
Merrion St, entrance at Kildare St. Tel: (01) 618 3000. Open when Parliament is in session – phone ahead for details of permission for entry.

Mansion House

The Mansion House is the official residence of the Lord Mayor of Dublin. The Round Room inside was the assembly room of the first Dáil Eireann and where, in 1919, the Declaration of Independence was ratified.
Dawson St. Closed to the public.

Molly Malone statue

The famous Dublin character with her wheelbarrow is at the lower end of Grafton St. Jean Rhynhart was the sculptor.

On Grafton St, near the junction with Suffolk St.

National Library of Ireland

The interior of this library is a massive dome towering over a room which is filled with period oak panelling, old-fashioned desks with green lamps and old bookshelves. The ancient books in the library are filled with the history and customs of Ireland that provided source material for many generations of writers and great thinkers. There is a genealogical office for those who have a little Irish blood in them.

Kildare St. Tel: (01) 603 0200. Email: info@nli.ie. www.nli.ie. Open: Mon–Wed 9.30am–9pm, Thur–Fri 9.30am–5pm, Sat 9.30am–1pm. Closed: Sun. Free admission.

Bewley's is a Grafton St landmark

Kilmainham

Just a short distance from Dublin city centre, Kilmainham was one of the locations where the Vikings first settled and built one of their longphorts. There was a Christian abbey here before the Vikings arrived and it is believed that the Vikings sacked the abbey and took it over for themselves. Kilmainham is also home to the infamous gaol and the Royal Hospital, which has been converted into the Irish Museum of Modern Art.

The Irish Museum of Modern Art (IMMA)

The Royal Hospital Kilmainham is 2.5km (1½ miles) west of the city centre. At the time of its construction the site was part of Phoenix Park. Designed in 1690 as a home for invalided soldiers, it was the first major public building to be constructed in Dublin. It was built on the site of a much older large hospital founded by the first Norman leader, Strongbow, and under the care of the Knights of St John of Jerusalem.

The design of the hospital by Sir William Robinson (he also designed Marsh's Library) was based on Les Invalides Hospital in Paris. Robinson was commissioned by James Butler, the Duke of Ormond and Viceroy, who was very impressed by the Parisian hospital.

It was such an impressive building when built that it was suggested it should be the campus for Trinity College, but the college stayed on its present site at College Green. In 1927 the hospital closed and became the Garda Headquarters from 1930 to 1950.

After this the building fell into disrepair until it was restored in the 1980s. The residential quarters of the former hospital were redesigned to house the Irish Museum of Modern Art (IMMA) in 1991. It is the foremost gallery for contemporary art in Ireland. There are guided tours of the North Range, which is also hired out by IMMA for banquets.

The exhibition programme includes Irish and international art by historical figures, as well as by established and younger-generation artists in retrospectives, solo and group exhibitions, each lasting approximately 3–4 months.

The New Galleries – a series of climate-controlled galleries housing exhibits from significant international collections – were opened to the public at IMMA in 2000. They are situated in

Sculpture outside the IMMA

the former Deputy Master's House, adjacent to the Formal Garden in the northeast corner of the Royal Hospital site.

Royal Hospital, Military Rd, Kilmainham. Tel: (01) 612 9900. www.imma.ie. Open: Tue–Sat 10am–5.30pm, Sun & Public Holidays noon–5.30pm. Closed: Mon. Free admission. Bus: 26, 51, 79, 90.

Bully's Acre

The monastery that the Vikings sacked, which dated from the late 6th century, was that of St Maighniu. He gave the area its name, Cill Mhaighnean, which was anglicised to Kilmainham. A Viking cemetery was uncovered here. Some of the graves are in the traditional Norse burial style, but there are also Christian-type burials, which indicates that some of the Vikings converted to Christianity.

The graveyard can be found in the grounds of the IMMA.

Kilmainham Gaol

This prison was built in 1795 and was the site of imprisonment of all the major uprising leaders since then.

The interior of Kilmainham Gaol

Kilmainham is one of the last 'urban' villages

Robert Emmet and Charles Stewart Parnell stayed here. But its role in the imprisonment of the leaders of the 1916 Easter Rising is etched most painfully in the memory of most Irish people.

Of the fifteen executions of the leaders of the Rising, fourteen were carried out here. The shooting of the badly injured James Connolly, who had to be strapped to a chair, was particularly cruel. Joseph Plunkett, another leader of the Rising, was married in the chapel just before he was shot. The last prisoner in the gaol was Eamonn DeValera, who later became Taoiseach and the President of Ireland. Dev, also affectionately called 'The Long Man' because of his height,

played an active role in the 1916 Easter Rising. In the 1960s the building was restored and opened as a museum. The tour takes you through the Georgian parts of the gaol where prisoners were kept in shockingly cramped conditions and on to the Victorian wing – which may look familiar to some as it was used in films such as *In the Name of the Father*.

Inchicore Rd. Tel: (01) 453 5984.
Open: Apr–Sept daily 9.30am–6pm (last admission 4.45pm); Oct–Mar Mon–Sat 9.30am–5.30pm (last admission 4pm), Sun 10am–6pm (last admission 4.45pm). Last tour 1 hour before closing. Admission by tour only.
Bus: 51B, 51C, 78A, 79.

Music and dance

The Irish music scene is strong and music plays an important part in a Dubliner's life. From the traditional through pop to rock, Irish bands are right up there with the top international acts. Dublin is one of the most important music cities in the world.

You are unlikely to associate Dublin with classical music, but in the 18th century the city was quite a draw for European composers. The greatest claim to a classical musical heritage Dublin has is the fact that George Frideric Handel composed and premiered his most famous work, *The Messiah*, when he was staying in the city. It is thought he composed

Street musicians are a common sight in Dublin

the work on the organ in St Michan's Church. The performance, on 13 April 1742, was by the collective choirs of Christ Church and St Patrick's cathedrals at the old Music Hall in Fishamble St. The Music Hall is long gone and a hotel has taken the composer's name in its place.

The contribution of Irish bands, particularly those from Dublin, to the international rock scene has been considerable through the years. U2 is the most famous Dublin band and the most successful Irish act ever. The four band members – Bono, The Edge, Adam Clayton and Larry Mullins – are all Dublin born and bred and still all live in the city, albeit in the suburbs.

The individualistic vocalist Sinéad O'Connor is also a Dubliner. In the 1990s she was controversial for her outspoken remarks, but there is no doubting her talent. As well as her success in the rock world, she performs some incredible versions of traditional songs, including the distinctive unaccompanied singing of former times called *Sean nós* singing.

Bob Geldof also hails from the city, and although he did achieve considerable success with his band The Boomtown Rats, his greatest claim to fame was the organisation of

Although associated with Scotland, the bagpipes are also a feature of Irish traditional music

the Live Aid event (in 1985) as an Ethiopian famine appeal and the Live 8 event (in 2005) to highlight the plight of the poorest nations in the world. He has received a knighthood from the British realm.

Love them or hate them, Westlife have been one of the most popular phenomena in commercial pop music. Dublin band Boyzone set the tune for Irish success in this arena. Ronan Keating, a member of Boyzone, has also enjoyed a successful solo career. Less well known, but doing nicely, are The Frames, Samantha Mumba, Damien Rice and David Kitt.

Many of Ireland's famous musicians have resided in Dublin over the years and include Van Morrison, The Corrs and The Cranberries.

Dublin traditional (trad) bands have made a considerable contribution to the revival of traditional Irish music.

The international success and well-deserved acclaim of The Chieftains and The Dubliners have brought Irish music to a whole new worldwide audience. For years Irish trad music was only played in a select group of Dublin pubs or in rural Ireland. Now the trad music scene is strong in Dublin. Some of the venues where music is played have become a little touristy and can be very crowded, especially in Temple Bar in the evenings and at weekends. The best trad sessions are when an impromptu collection of musicians take out their instruments and play some unrehearsed songs. The professional musicians are paid in Euros to perform in the touristy venues (they used to be paid in pints). Many of the pubs where the best music is played are kept secret by the locals, so you will need to twist someone's arm to get them to take you there.

The Eurovision Song Contest has launched more than a few music careers, and Bill Whelan, composer of the interval performance at the event when it was based in Dublin in 1994, did not realise the effect that his work would have. After the seven-minute performance, his work was an overnight sensation and Riverdance was born. The fusion of traditional Celtic dancing with modern dance has achieved worldwide recognition and fame and a million knock-offs.

Walk: a musical stroll

This walk embraces Dublin's musical heritage. It takes you to some of the places that launched the careers of Dublin's most famous rock stars and to the site where Handel's Messiah *was first publicly performed.*

Allow 1½ hours.

The walk starts at Pearse Station.
Turn right, cross Pearse St and go down Lombard St East. Turn right into Townsend St and then go left and right into Windmill Lane.

1 Windmill Lane

This is the home of the original Windmill Lane Studios, opened in 1978, where many of U2's early albums were cut. The 'Wall' outside is covered in graffiti dedicated to the band.
Return to Pearse St and walk all the way to Dame St past the main entrance to Trinity. Just before the Central Bank on the right, walk into Temple Bar down Crown Alley.

2 Eamon Doran's Bar

The Cranberries played their first gig on this site, the old Rock Garden venue.
Turn left into Temple Bar and right through Merchant's Arch.

3 Merchant's Arch

Phil Lynott used to busk here before he became lead singer of Thin Lizzy.

Turn left and walk along Wellington Quay. At the end is the Clarence Hotel.

4 The Clarence

Once a small, run-down hotel and bar, this is one of the places where the then-unknown Bono and his friends sat and planned out their futures. They bought it in 1992 and have turned it into a luxury hotel.
Continue along the quays and turn left into Bridgefoot St. Turn left again into Thomas St.

5 St Catherine's Church, Thomas St

The most famous Irish traditional band, The Chieftains, played their first gig in this church.
Walk along Thomas St. At the top of Lord Edward St, turn left into Fishamble St.

6 Fishamble St

An hotel now stands on the site of the Music Hall where Handel's *Messiah* was first performed.

Return to Lord Edward St and walk to College Green. Turn right on Suffolk St and right to Grafton St.

7 Bewley's, Grafton St

The Boomtown Rats used to meet in Bewley's Coffee Shop and it is where Bob Geldof penned his most famous song, *Rat Trap*.

8 Dunne's

The opening scenes of the movie *Once* (2007), written and directed by Irish film director John Carney, were filmed secretly outside Dunne's Stores. The movie tells the story of a local musician, played by Glen Hansard (of Dublin band The Frames), and a

Czech girl, played by Markéta Irglová, a Czech musician now living in Dublin.

9 Statue of Phil Lynott

On Harry St there is a new statue in tribute to Phil Lynott.

10 Captain Americas, Grafton St

Chris DeBurgh launched his solo career from here.
Walk along Stephen's Green West and then right around Stephen's Green till you come to Merrion Row.

11 O'Donoghues, Merrion Row

The traditional band, The Dubliners, formed here in the back bar in 1962. This is one of the best live venues.

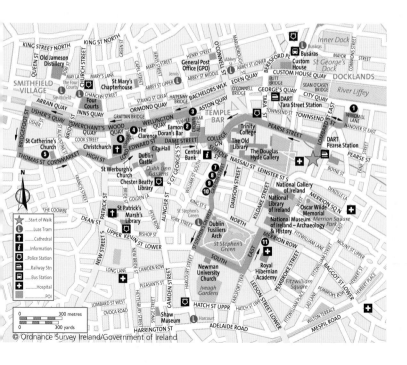

© Ordnance Survey Ireland/Government of Ireland

Literary Dublin

The literary heritage of Dublin city is the envy of every other city in the world. There have been three Nobel Prizes for Literature awarded to Dubliners. The place is positively bursting with literary talent even today, with many Dublin poets, novelists and playwrights having achieved worldwide fame and recognition.

Dublin has an internationally acclaimed tradition in theatre and you would be hard pushed to find a city anywhere with such a strong theatrical heritage. The Smock Alley Theatre, which opened in 1662, was the first in Dublin. It was notorious for its provocative plays, which invariably ended in a riot and often bloodshed.

Abbey Theatre

Founded by W B Yeats, Lady Gregory and George Russell (who wrote under the pseudonym 'AE') in 1904.

In 1907 J M Synge's *Playboy of the Western World* was the first play to cause consternation at the Abbey. The audience objected most strongly to the word 'shift', which in those days meant undergarment, and to the fact that the main character boasted about having killed his father. The riots were so bad that the police had to intervene.

The next great playwright to cause controversy was Sean O'Casey, and when his play *The Plough and the Stars* premiered in 1926 there were riots again. The problem was that O'Casey had dared to suggest that there were prostitutes in Dublin, which was unthinkable at the time. On the fifth night, Yeats faced the audience and remonstrated: 'Is this going to be a recurring celebration of Irish genius? Synge first, and then O'Casey. Dublin once more has rocked the cradle of a reputation.' O'Casey left Dublin disenchanted, like many of the city's greatest writers.
26 Lower Abbey St. Tel: (01) 878 7222. www.abbeytheatre.ie

Dublin Writers' Museum

Housed in an elegant Georgian house, this museum pays tribute to Dublin's historical literary greats. All of the best writers of note are represented with their books, letters, and some photographs and personal items. There is a room devoted to children's literature. They sometimes have readings or lectures.

18 Parnell Square. Tel: (01) 872 2077. www.writersmuseum.com. Open: Mon–Sat 10am–5pm. Sun & Public Holidays 11am–5pm; Jun–Aug Mon–Fri late opening until 6pm. Admission charge.

Gate Theatre

Housed in part of the Rotunda Hospital. The partnership of Hilton Edwards and Michael MacLiammoir helped to launch this theatre, which was the early stomping ground of such greats as Orson Welles and James Mason.

Cavendish Row, Parnell Square. Tel: (01) 874 4045. www.gate-theatre.ie

The Olympia Theatre

The Olympia is the oldest existing Dublin theatre, dating from the 1870s. Peadar Kearney, creator of the Irish National Anthem, turned a fire hose on the audience when the British national anthem was played here.

72 Dame St. Tel: (01) 679 3323.

Shaw Museum

No 33 Synge St is the birthplace of George Bernard Shaw, the author of *Pygmalion* (on which the musical *My Fair Lady* is based) and *St Joan* (for which he received the Nobel Prize for Literature). The plaque on the wall outside his birthplace is unbelievably understated ('Author of many plays'), for the talents of the man were truly immense. The home of the Shaw family is a simple Victorian house and gives an insight into his early life.

33 Synge St. Tel: (01) 475 0854. Open: May–Sept Mon–Fri 10am–1pm, 2–5pm (closed Wed), Sat, Sun & Public Holidays 2–5pm. Admission charge. Ten minutes' walk from St Stephen's Green. Bus: 16, 19, 122 from city centre.

The grand façade of The Olympia

Dublin's greatest writers

This list is not exhaustive, but gives you an idea of the amount of literary talent that the city has produced.

Samuel Beckett (1906–89)

Nobel Prize winner. Author and playwright. Some of his most famous works include *Waiting for Godot*, *Krapp's Last Tape* and *Endgame.*

Brendan Behan (1923–64)

The quintessential Dubliner and literary drunk. Frequently banned from many of Dublin's pubs. Author of *Borstal Boy* and *The Quare Fellow.*

Maeve Binchy (1940–)

Best-selling author of *Circle of Friends*, *Tara Road* and *The Lilac Bus.*

Dermot Bolger (1959–)

Author of *The Journey Home*, which details a darker side of Dublin City.

Roddy Doyle (1958–)

Booker Prize winner. Author of *Paddy Clarke Ha Ha Ha* and *The Commitments*, which was subsequently a success on the silver screen.

James Joyce (1882–1941)

The most famous of Dublin novelists. Author of *Ulysses*, *Finnegan's Wake*, *Portrait of the Artist as a Young Man* and *Dubliners.*

Patrick Kavanagh (1904–67)

Poet from County Monaghan who lived in Dublin. His poem *On Raglan Road* was put to music by the

Exterior of the Abbey Theatre, home to many productions by local playwrights

Oscar Wilde in repose in Merrion Square

traditional Irish music band The Dubliners.

Martin McDonagh (1970–)

Author of innovative dramas such as *The Pillowman*, and movies such as *Six Shooter* (which won an Oscar in 2006) and *In Bruges*. Of Irish descent, his play *The Beauty Queen of Leenane* was premiered in Dublin (and subsequently went on to Broadway).

Thomas Moore (1779–1852)

Romantic lyricist best known for the lyrics of *The Minstrel Boy* and *The Last Rose of Summer*.

Flann O'Brien (1911–66)

Brilliant comic writer who has not yet received the recognition he deserves.

Author of *The Dalkey Archive, At Swim-Two-Birds* and *The Third Policeman*.

Sean O'Casey (1880–1964)

Playwright. Author of *The Plough and the Stars, The Shadow of a Gunman* and *Juno and the Paycock*.

George Bernard Shaw (1856–1950)

Nobel Prize-winning playwright. Author of *Pygmalion* (later adapted as the musical *My Fair Lady*) and *St Joan*.

Bram Stoker (1847–1912)

Horror novelist. Author of *Dracula*.

Jonathan Swift (1667–1745)

Satirical writer and novelist. Author of *Gulliver's Travels*.

J M Synge (1871–1909)

Playwright. Author of *Playboy of the Western World*.

Oscar Fingal O'Flahertie Wills Wilde (1854–1900)

Playwright. Author of *Lady Windermere's Fan, The Importance of Being Earnest* and his masterpiece poem, *The Ballad of Reading Gaol*.

W B Yeats (1865–1935)

Ireland's favourite poet and Nobel Prize winner. Some of his most famous poems include *The Lake Isle of Innisfree, He Wishes for the Cloths of Heaven* and *The Song of Wandering Aengus*. Co-founder of the Abbey Theatre.

Joycean Dublin

James Joyce is Dublin's most famous author. He produced two of the most complex and revolutionary novels in the English language – *Ulysses* and *Finnegan's Wake*. Joyce is the literary son of whom Dubliners are proudest, even though most have never read him and would find his greatest work, *Ulysses*, impenetrable.

James Joyce was born in 1882, the eldest of ten children. He went to school at Belvedere College on Great Denmark St, and then attended University College Dublin. Although all of Joyce's stories are based in Dublin, he himself became disenchanted with the city. Joyce had a love–hate relationship with his homeland and particularly with the city where he was born. He wrote 'This lovely land that always sent Her writers and artists to banishment.' He left Dublin forever at the age of 22.

He went on to live in Trieste, Zurich, Paris and finally back to Zurich where he died in 1941. He is buried there.

Joyce's work was all about Dublin and in his mind he never really left the city.

His ambitions are summed up in *Ulysses*: 'I want to give a picture of Dublin so complete that if the city suddenly one day disappeared from the earth it could be reconstructed out of my book.' Based on a day in the life of its two main characters Stephen Dedalus and Leopold Bloom, *Ulysses* provides an insight into Dublin on one day: 16 June 1904. Joyce linked the events of the day to Homer's *Odyssey*. *Ulysses* is often described as a 'stream of consciousness' book and it is quite difficult to read. In fact, it has been called 'the great unread work of the English language'.

However, every year on 16 June, Bloomsday is celebrated. Dressed in period costume, Dubliners recreate on the streets the events of the day in *Ulysses*. The tradition was started on the 50th anniversary of the day in the book by a group of Dublin writers including Patrick Kavanagh and Flann O'Brien.

The action of *Ulysses* begins at the Martello tower where Joyce lived briefly during his student days. The tower, renamed **Joyce's Tower**, now contains a museum and you can see some of his manuscripts and personal belongings and some rare editions of his books. In the book it was referred to as the 'omphalos' or 'navelstone of the universe'.

Joyce's Tower, Sandycove, Co. Dublin. Tel & Fax: (01) 280 9265.

Open: Mar–Oct Mon–Sat 10am–1pm
& 2–5pm, Sun & Public Holidays
2–6pm; Nov–Feb open by
arrangement. Admission charge.

The James Joyce Centre is a
restored Georgian house which used
to belong to a character who
appeared in *Ulysses* briefly. It contains
various personal items of Joyce's,
including his piano, some family
photos, books and manuscripts. The
door of No 7 Eccles St, the home of
Leopold Bloom in *Ulysses*, is also on
display. The centre organises walking
tours of Joycean locations in Dublin.
35 North Great George's St.
Tel: (01) 878 8547. Fax: (01) 878 8488.
Email: info@jamesjoyce.ie.
www.jamesjoyce.ie. Open: Tue–Sat
10am–5pm. Closed: Sun & Mon,
1 Jan, Good Friday, 24–31 Dec.
Admission charge.

Joyce – the hick with the stick

Walk: literary Dublin

Our literary walk around Dublin combines both fiction and reality. You will really get a feel for the magnitude of writing talent that the city has produced, and the walk takes in some of the haunts of Dublin's best writers.

The walk starts at Great George's St. Allow 2 hours.

1 James Joyce Centre
(*See p71.*)
Turn left into Great Denmark St and continue until you reach Parnell Square.

2 Dublin Writers' Museum
(*See pp66–7.*)
Continue down O'Connell St.

3 James Joyce's statue
In Dublin's inimitable style, the locals call it the 'hick with the stick'.
Turn left at Earl St North and right on Marlborough St.

4 Abbey Theatre
(*See p66.*)
Turn right onto Eden Quay and cross the Liffey at O'Connell Bridge. Walk along Westmoreland St and turn left into Nassau St and Clare St to Merrion Square. Go into the park.

5 Merrion Square
Oscar Wilde's home is at No 1 Merrion Square East. W B Yeats also lived in the square, at No 82, as did John Sheridan Le Fanu, a writer of horror fiction.
Walk down Merrion St and turn right into Merrion Row, then left into St Stephen's Green East. Turn left into Leeson St to the canal, then left into Wilton Terrace.

6 Patrick Kavanagh statue
Seated on a bench is a sculpture of the poet Patrick Kavanagh, who often frequented the banks of the Grand Canal.
Go back along the canal to Camden St, then turn right. Turn left into Harrington St and right into Synge St.

7 Shaw Museum, 33 Synge St
Shaw's birthplace has been transformed into a museum (*see p67*).
Turn right towards Camden Row and left then right into Bride St. Turn left at Kevin St Upper and right into Patrick St.

8 St Patrick's Cathedral
(*See p43.*)
Turn right at Bull Alley and continue straight until you reach William St South.

Turn right and then left down Chatham Row and then left into Balfe St.

Turn left into Grafton St and then right into Duke St.

9 McDaids

A famous literary pub.

3 Harry St. Tel: (01) 679 4395.

10 Davy Byrnes

This is Joyce's 'Moral Pub'.

21 Duke St. Tel: (01) 677 5217.

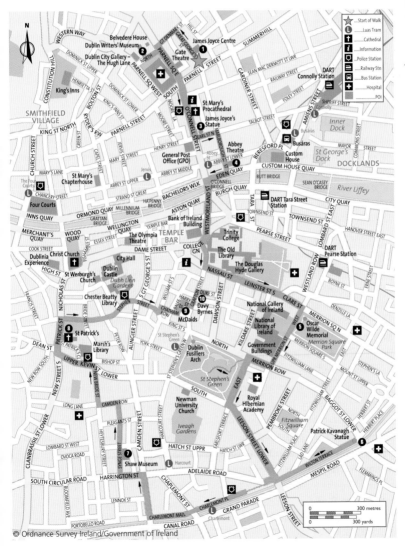

© Ordnance Survey Ireland/Government of Ireland

National Gallery and the visual arts

In Ireland the visual arts are probably the most underdeveloped of the arts and have been sadly neglected. Jack B Yeats, W B Yeats' brother, is the best known artist. Francis Bacon was also Irish and born in Dublin. Some of Ireland's modern visual artists have achieved considerable international acclaim but remain relatively unknown in their own country.

National Gallery of Ireland

There is a considerable collection of Western European art dating from the Middle Ages in this foremost gallery of art in the country. Depending on where you enter the National Gallery, you might think that you are entering two entirely different galleries. The old entrance on Merrion Square West leads you into the part of the gallery that opened in the late 19th century and has a distinctly Georgian feel. The new entrance on Clare St, the Millennium Wing, has won awards for its architectural innovation. It has fascinating little alcoves with a clever use of space – almost works of art in themselves. It is arguably the most attractive modern building in the city and is a pleasant place to have a sandwich and a coffee. In the Milltown wing you can view some of the work of the most famous of Irish artists, including Jack B Yeats.
Clare St/Merrion Square West. Tel: (01) 661 5133. Email: info@ngi.ie.

www.nationalgallery.ie. Open: Mon–Sat 9.30am–5.30pm, Thur 9.30am–8.30pm, Sun noon–5.30pm. Free admission, but there is a charge for certain exhibitions. Free public tours: Sat 3pm, Sun 2pm, 3pm & 4pm. DART: Pearse station (Westland Row) is a 5-minute walk from the National Gallery.

Dublin City Gallery – The Hugh Lane

The Hugh Lane contains a fascinating and comprehensive collection of contemporary Irish art from the 20th century and some Impressionist masterpieces. Designed by William Chambers, Charlemont House is one of the most attractive buildings in Dublin. It was sold to the government in 1870, becoming the General Register, and in 1933 the gallery moved here. Sir Hugh Lane, the wealthy nephew of Lady Gregory, was an art collector. He donated some of his incredible collection to the Dublin gallery, but he was not happy with the way he was treated in Ireland.

He drowned in 1915 when the *Lusitania* was sunk by the torpedoes of a German U-boat.

Because of a dispute over his will, the Hugh Lane Collection is shared between The Hugh Lane Gallery in Dublin and the National Gallery in London.

Charlemont House, Parnell Square North. Tel: (01) 222 5550. www.hughlane.ie. Open: Tue–Thur 10am–6pm, Fri–Sat 10am–5pm, Sun 11am–5pm. Closed: Mon. Free admission. The gallery is a short walk from the city centre and only a 5-minute walk from O'Connell St. Bus: 3, 7, 10, 11, 13, 16, 19, 46A, 123 pass close to the Hugh Lane Gallery. DART: Connolly station or Tara St station. It is equidistant from both and a 10-minute walk.

The Francis Bacon Studio

The undoubted highlight of the Hugh Lane Gallery is the Francis Bacon Studio. The studio is a replica of the one the famous Dublin painter worked in for over 30 years, producing his extraordinary body of work. It consists of the artist's reconstructed studio, an audiovisual room showing a videoed interview with British TV presenter Melvyn Bragg, and some of his unfinished works. It provides a fascinating insight into the mind of the artist and how he worked.

Other galleries

Other Dublin galleries of particular note include the Irish Museum of Modern Art (*see pp58–60*), the **Royal Hibernian Academy** (*15 Ely Place. Tel: (01) 661 2558. Open: Tue–Sat 11am–5pm, Thur until 8pm, Sun 2–5pm. Closed: Mon. Free admission*) and **The Douglas Hyde Gallery** (*Trinity College. Tel: (01) 896 1116. Open: Mon–Fri 11am–6pm, Thur until 7pm, Sat 11am–4.45pm. Closed: Sun. Free admission*).

National Gallery and the visual arts

The façade of the National Gallery of Ireland

National museums

There are three main museums to see in Dublin: Collins Barracks, The National Archaeology Museum at Kildare St and the Natural History Museum (www.museum.ie). They are all managed by the state, are free to visit, and they provide a valuable insight into the history, culture and treasures of Ireland.

National Museum of Ireland – Archaeology & History

This museum is housed in one of the most beautiful buildings in the country. Apart from the excellence of the exhibits on show, the ambience of the surroundings will truly amaze you. You will discover some intricately carved wooden panelling and incredibly detailed stucco decoration as you wander around.

The **Treasury Exhibition** features examples of Celtic and medieval art including an outstanding display of Irish gold treasures. The works in the gold collection are the most outstanding examples of Bronze Age and medieval metalwork anywhere in the world. Two must-sees from this collection are the **Ardagh Chalice** and the **Tara Brooch**. The Ardagh Chalice was made to dispense the Sacrament during Mass and dates from the 8th century. It was found near Ardagh in County Limerick and was probably deliberately buried to prevent it getting into Viking hands. The Tara Brooch dates from AD 700 and was found near the River Boyne. The detail of the animal decoration on the white bronze brooch is exquisite.

The Viking section of the museum is particularly poignant as these remains were excavated from Wood Quay. The Vikings introduced town settlements to Ireland and founded Dublin. The site of the excavation at Wood Quay is where the new Dublin Corporation Offices are currently situated and there was a public outcry when the building was constructed on the top of the old Viking settlement that was the site of the birth of Dublin. But progress won the day and the ancient site was destroyed to make way for the new offices. From the exhibits we can see that the Vikings were not as ferocious and uncivilised as they were made out to be. They made a considerable contribution to the social and cultural fabric of society and completely integrated into the population over time. Many of them became Christians. The medieval section of the museum is also excellent and, combined with a visit to Dublinia, provides an excellent insight into early and medieval Dublin.

Kildare St. Open: Tue–Sat 10am–5pm, Sun 2–5pm. Closed: Mon & Public Holidays. Free admission, charge for tour. Getting there: short walk from the centre of town and very close to Grafton St. Bus: 7, 7A and 8 all leave the town centre from Burgh Quay. DART: Pearse station (Westland Row). It is about a 10-minute walk. Cookes Café is in the museum if you feel like some refreshment or a break from studying the exhibits.

National Museum of Ireland – Decorative Arts & History/ Collins Barracks

Formerly a military barracks, this site has been completely renovated and two sides now house the National Museum of Decorative Arts & History.

The objects on display range from weaponry, furniture, folklife and costume, to silver, ceramics and glassware. The design of the museum is contemporary and there is portable seating for those who get weary limbs after a while. The **Airgead Exhibition** is the currency collection and it features coinage from medieval times to the modern day. The Vikings introduced coins to Ireland in the 10th century and

National museums

The Ardagh Chalice, part of the Treasury Exhibition

The Collins Barracks have been converted into a National Museum

there are examples of these first coins. Some other highlights include rare gold coins from the 1640s, the 'gunmoney' of King James II and plastic moulds used to cast the first Free State coins in 1928. The poet W B Yeats helped to choose the designs for the new Republic's first currency. There are also examples of Victorian silverware, early furniture and period weaponry.

Collins Barracks, Benburb St.
Tel: (01) 677 7444. www.museum.ie.
Open: Tue–Sat 10am–5pm, Sun 2–5pm.
Closed: Mon & Public Holidays. Free
admission, charge for tour. Getting there:
a good 15–20-minute walk from the
centre of Dublin. Bus: 90, 25, 25A, 66,
67. It is located on the Northside of the
Liffey. Luas: Museum.

National Museum of Ireland – Natural History

For 150 years one of the highlights of the national museums has been the Natural History Museum, set in its purpose-built house and virtually untouched for all that time. Known affectionately as the 'Dead Zoo', the place was filled with looming skeletons and beautiful Victorian display cases filled with all manner of creatures, some of them now extinct. Two collections distinguished between native fauna and specimens collected by enthusiastic

Victorians from around the world. In 2007 a staircase collapsed in the museum, narrowly missing some visitors, and so the museum has been temporarily removed to a little wing of the Collins Barracks site. Much reduced in size, it is still a fascinating and somewhat gruesome place to visit. The megaloceros, a giant elk, is still there, looking like it is waiting for a ringwraith from *The Lord of the Rings* to mount it. Lots of stuffed creatures are frozen in time in the display cases, and there are some exquisite fossils and shells. Look out for the head of an Atlantic halibut, bigger than the bear skull that is set beside it. Alongside the exhibits are the plans for the renovation of the old site, and a touchy feely room where there are regular talks given on wildlife. As of late 2009 there was no set date for reopening the Merrion Street building, but work is clearly in progress and you can peer in through the railings by the statue of T H Parke, who no doubt contributed many of the building's occupants to the collection.

Collins Barracks, Benburb St.
Tel: (01) 677 7444. www.museum.ie.
Open: Tue–Sat 10am–5pm, Sun 2–5pm.
Closed: Mon & Public Holidays. Free admission, charge for tour. Getting there: a good 15–20-minute walk from the centre of Dublin. Bus: 90, 25, 25A, 66, 67. It is located on the Northside of the Liffey. Luas: Museum.

Irish explorer T H Parke stands guard outside the original home of the 'Dead Zoo'

The Liffey

The Liffey is no longer a very wide river nor is it very deep, but it is the lifeblood of Dublin City and is beloved by all Dubliners. The River Liffey is seen as female and her name is Anna Livia, from the Irish Abha Liphe or the 'river of Liphe', which was the name of a plain the river flowed through on her way to the sea. She has been immortalised in literature by her most famous literary son, James Joyce, in Finnegan's Wake, *as Anna Livia. Mr Joyce added the word Plurabelle, which means 'most lovely'.*

For centuries the banks of the Liffey have been neglected and it is only now, with Dublin's redevelopment, that the river is being used as part of the commercial and social structure of the city. The Liffey was much wider in former times and has only been enclosed behind walls in the city since the 18th century. Before that, naturally estuarial, it ebbed and flowed with the tide. Although it may look dirty, it is much cleaner than it was previously and the silt-carrying turbidity is a natural phenomenon of tidal rivers.

Custom House

This is the most beautiful Georgian building in Dublin and is sited on the riverfront with Beresford Place to the rear. The first major public building built in Dublin, the Custom House is an isolated structure with four monumental façades. A previous Custom House stood upriver and the local merchants were against moving the centre of the economy further east because they felt it would lower the value of their property. However, the Chief Commissioner, John Beresford, pushed the project and asked architect James Gandon to build it.

The Custom House was built on reclaimed land from the Liffey and took ten years to complete at a cost of £200,000. The building was gutted in an extensive fire started by the IRA during the War of Independence in 1921, but it has since been renovated. The visitor centre displays information about the architect James Gandon and his life, the restoration after the 1921 fire and also various famous personalities who have worked in the offices in the past.

Custom House Quay.
Tel: (01) 888 2538.
Fax: (01) 888 2407. Open: mid-Mar–Oct Mon–Fri 10am–12.30pm, Sat–Sun 2–5pm; Nov–mid-Mar Wed–Fri

10–12.30pm, Sun 2–5pm.
Closed: Sat, Mon & Tue.
Free admission. Short walk from the
city centre, about a 5-minute walk
east from O'Connell Bridge, and a
5-minute walk from Busaras station.
DART: Tara St station.

Liffey boardwalk

The new Liffey boardwalks and the two new bridges have given new life to the banks of the river where pedestrianised streets, cycle paths, artworks and pleasant seating make the river an attraction in itself.

The Liffey

The new Sean O'Casey Bridge across the Liffey

Walk: a stroll along the River Liffey

This walk starts from the O₂ (formerly the Point Depot) but you can start from St George's Dock in the Docklands. The River Liffey flows through the heart of the city and this walk takes you right along the banks of the river.

Take Bus No 90 to the O₂. Allow 2 hours.

1 O₂

This converted railway goods depot is now the premier rock venue.
Tel: (01) 676 6144.
Box office: (081) 871 9391.
Walk along the North Wall Quay.

2 Sean O'Casey Bridge

The newest footbridge over the Liffey has become a welcome link with the south side of the river.
Continue to Docklands and turn left.

3 Famine statues

These pay tribute to those who died in the Great Famine of the 1840s.

Turn right into St George's Dock through an alleyway opposite the statues.

4 St George's Dock

The Stack A warehouse redevelopment into a cultural centre and the National Conference Centre have rejuvenated the area.
Turn left on Mayor St and then walk around to Amiens St where you turn left. Turn left on Beresford Place, then right on to Custom House Quay.

5 Custom House

(See pp80–81.)
Continue along Custom House Quay.

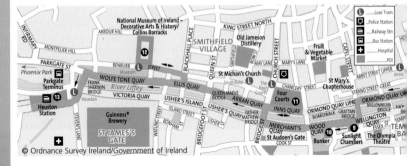

© Ordnance Survey Ireland/Government of Ireland

6 Liberty Hall

The tallest building in Dublin.
Return to the Liffey. Cross Butt Bridge. This part of the walk is optional. Turn right up Burgh Quay. Continue alongside the river.

7 O'Connell Bridge

The unusual feature of the busiest of Dublin's bridges is that it is almost square.
Continue west along Aston Quay.

8 Ha'penny Bridge

The city's emblematic bridge was restored to its former glory with a thorough clean in 2001.
Cross the bridge to the Northside of the river and walk along the boardwalk in a westerly direction. Cross Grattan Bridge to Southside and continue walking west.

9 Sunlight Chambers

The terracotta friezes on this building depict the history of soap manufacture.
Continue westwards.

10 Bunker

The Dublin Corporation Offices were dubbed the 'Bunker' because of the completely unimaginative design.
Continue along the quay and turn right on Fr Mathew Bridge and right along Inns Quay.

11 Four Courts

This was architect James Gandon's second great building on the Northside (the other being the Custom House).
Walk along Arran Quay, then turn right off Ellis Quay, then left on Benburb St.

12 Collins Barracks

The former army base was renovated in 1999 and is now the National Museum of Decorative Arts & History (*see pp77–8*).
Return to Ellis Quay and turn right. Cross the river via Frank Sherwin Bridge.

13 Heuston Station

Named after another Easter Rising rebel, Sean Heuston, this is the foremost railway station in Dublin.
Bus No 90 will take you back to the city centre.

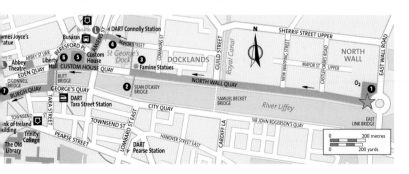

O'Connell Street

The city's main thoroughfare dates back to the early 18th century. It was called Drogheda St by Viscount Henry Moore, the Earl of Drogheda. He was the city's official street namer, and Henry St and Moore St stand testament to this. In 1740 it was bought by aristocrat Luke Gardiner, who later became Viscount Mountjoy. He widened the street and envisaged a grand residential parade with an elegant mall. The street was renamed Gardiner's Mall, but it never became the boulevard Gardiner desired.

O'Connell St has witnessed some of Dublin's most historic moments.

Apart from the Easter Rising of 1916, which centred around the General Post Office, there was the blowing up of Nelson's column in 1966. The column, which predated the one in Trafalgar Square, was always seen as a symbol of British imperialism and the explosion was on the anniversary of the Easter Rising.

Since the beginning of the 20th century, the grand, broad sweep of O'Connell St has been sadly neglected and little of the original architecture remains. There are many bland functional buildings, often housing burger bars. However, ambitious plans are afoot for the regeneration of O'Connell St and the creation of a new street to make Dublin proud. The street has thankfully had its traffic flow much reduced by a clever semi-pedestrianisation scheme which has allowed some of the generous width of the street to shine through again,

and then of course there is the new Spire (*see opposite*).

General Post Office (GPO)

The GPO was built in 1814 and designed by architect Francis Johnston. More than any other building in Dublin, the GPO is associated with the struggle for independence from the British. It was the headquarters for the doomed 1916

THE LIBERATOR AND HIS MONUMENT

O'Connell St was named after Daniel O'Connell the 'Liberator'. There is a monument to him at the entrance to O'Connell St. Erected in 1882, it features a statue of O'Connell at the top with four winged Victory statues at the base, representing the four provinces of Ireland. There are bullet holes left in them from the Easter Rising of 1916. O'Connell was a lawyer who achieved the Catholic Emancipation Act of 1829. The Act gave greater rights to Irish Catholics. O'Connell, who was also elected in 1840 as the first Catholic Mayor of Dublin, was a champion of human rights and instrumental in the abolition of slavery and anti-Semitism.

rebellion. It was practically destroyed in the Rising and the Irish Civil War, but was later renovated. The legendary Cúchulainn is commemorated inside.

The Spire

Completed in March 2003, the Monument of Light or The Spire is the newest (and highest) addition to the Dublin skyline. The Spire is the largest single piece of sculpture in the world and its reflective polished surface creates a new perspective on the street in Dublin's ever-changing light. The architect Ian Ritchie designed the 120m (394ft) high stainless steel spire and it is in the exact spot where Nelson's column stood.

O'Connell Bridge and The Spire in the background

The Easter Rising

The Easter Rising in 1916 was probably the most important event in Dublin's recent history. Although it was a doomed rebellion and there was no logical hope of success, it provided the psychological impetus for the Irish to gain eventual independence from the British (apart from the six counties that form Northern Ireland). Two thousand members of the Irish Citizens Army and the Irish Volunteers seized 14 key buildings in Dublin. There were 20,000 British troops. When the rebels finally surrendered, 64 of them had died, along with 134 police and soldiers and 200 civilians. Among the leaders of the Easter Rising were three poets with a romantic notion of attaining freedom for Ireland – Padraig Pearse, Thomas McDonagh and Joseph Mary Plunkett. The Rising started when on Easter Monday a group of volunteers left Liberty Hall and marched on the General Post Office. The Irish flag (green, white and orange tricolour) was raised above the building and Padraig Pearse went out on the street to read the Proclamation from the Provisional

The Irish flag flying high above the General Post Office

Façade of the General Post Office

Government of the Irish Republic to the People of Ireland. The plan was to seize several key buildings and use that as a platform to spark a revolution among the people, but it never happened and the rebellion was doomed before it even started. The rebels were outnumbered by three to one before the British Army brought in reinforcements. The fighting lasted for just a week and Pearse then ordered an unconditional surrender. Fifteen of the leaders of the Rising were executed in the following weeks, although two were spared. The first was Countess Markievicz, easily the most flamboyant and beautiful of the rebels, spared because she was a woman. She was from Anglo-Irish aristocracy and had been presented at court to Queen Victoria when she was only 19 years old. The second was Eamonn DeValera, who was spared because he had been born in America, even though he was the leader of one of the garrisons. He went on to be Ireland's longest-serving President. The Rising had a profound effect on the people of Ireland. The executed leaders are still considered to be heroes and perhaps their motivation and love of their country is best captured by W B Yeats in his poem 'Easter 1916':

'We know their dream; enough
To know they dreamed and are dead
And what if excess of love
Bewildered them till they died?'

Walk: the Northside

This walk is through the Northside of Dublin, and it gives a flavour of life north of the Liffey. Traditionally the neglected side of the Liffey, the Northside has in recent times been the focus of much of the city's redevelopment plan.

The walk starts at Connolly Station. Allow 1 hour.

1 Connolly Station

Originally known as Amiens St Station, it was built to the design of William Deane Butler for the Dublin to Drogheda Railway Company.
Walk down Talbot St to O'Connell St and turn left. Walk down the left-hand side of O'Connell Street until you reach O'Connell Bridge.

2 O'Connell St

The main street of Dublin is beginning to be restored to its former glory. The Spire has become a major landmark and tourist attraction. Look out for the statues of Dan O'Connell, and Jim Larkin with his outstretched hands.
Cross the road and retrace your steps back to Henry St. Turn left into Henry St, then right into Moore St.

3 & 4 Henry St and Moore St Market

Henry St is a busy shopping street for most of the year, but it really comes alive and bustles during the Christmas period. You will see some real Northsiders in the small but busy food market held daily on Moore St. Some of the produce still gets delivered to the market stalls by horse and cart.
Return to Henry St and continue down the road. Turn left into Jervis St and right into Abbey St Upper.

5 St Mary's Chapterhouse

This medieval abbey was built in 1139 but unfortunately little of it remains because the Green St Courthouse has now replaced the original building. There are still remains of the chapterhouse underground.
Turn right out of the abbey and turn right again into Church St. Turn left down May Lane and cross Bow St. At Bow St go into Smithfield.

6 Smithfield Village

Home of the Old Jameson Distillery and its chimney, Smithfield was famed for its Victorian market. The site has been redeveloped but still holds

Ireland's biggest horse market on the first Sunday of every month.
Go via King St North to Church St Upr. Go up Constitution Hill. Turn right into the King's Inns.

7 King's Inns

Built in 1817, this is a finely proportioned building. It was the last of architect James Gandon's public buildings, but he was not the only architect who worked on it – Francis Johnston added the cupola.
Pass through the arch to Henrietta St.

8 Henrietta St

This is the oldest of the remaining Georgian streets and it was laid out by architect Luke Gardiner in the 1720s.
Continue to the end of Henrietta St. Turn left into Bolton St and continue until Parnell Square West. Turn right.

9 Rotunda Hospital

The Rotunda Hospital was the first maternity hospital in Britain or Ireland. There were also social rooms called the Rotunda. The Round Room is now the Ambassador Cinema, the Supper Rooms are the Gate Theatre, and the Pillar Room is occasionally used for concerts. The Rotunda Chapel is the most important architectural feature of the hospital.
Continue down Parnell Square West and then turn left into Parnell Square South.

10 Parnell Monument

The monument to a former favourite political son of Ireland.

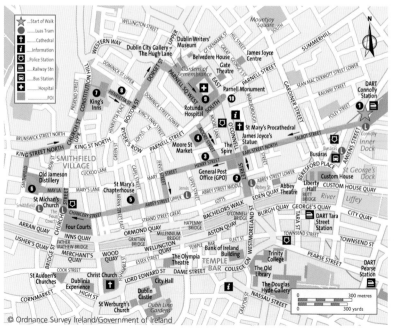

© Ordnance Survey Ireland/Government of Ireland

Smithfield

Smithfield is an area of regeneration. The home of the Victorian vegetable and horse markets is undergoing a face-lift. The vegetable market is to be transformed and the traditional horse market now has a considerably more slick, modern setting.

From an area of run-down, dilapidated housing, new apartment complexes, hotels and restaurants have been constructed. The government-appointed Historic Area Rejuvenation Plan (HARP) spearheaded the development. Smithfield Plaza is now a large civic plaza with restored cobbled paving and 25m (82ft) high braziers with gas-flamed beacons. The equine market on the first Sunday of every month sees the square fill up with hundreds of horses and dealers from all over Ireland and is an essential Dublin experience if you're there at the right time of month.

View from the top of Smithfield Chimney

Dublin City on Ice

The newest attraction in Smithfield is a Christmas ice rink in the style of the one at Rockefeller Plaza, New York. There is also a festive market.

Henrietta St

This is the oldest of the remaining Georgian streets and it was laid out by architect Luke Gardiner in the 1720s. Named after Henrietta, Duchess of Grafton, it is a dead end terminated by the Law Society's King's Inns and was designed as an enclave of prestigious houses.

The street is still cobbled but many of the fine houses are now in disrepair. In the mid-1700s the street was inhabited by many of Dublin's finest gentry. During the summer you may be able to view the interior of No 9 as the Sisters of Charity may let you in to have a peek around.

King's Inns

The King's Inns is the name of the collective group of people who represent the administration of the law in Ireland. The society, a kind of a posh trade union, was established in 1541, when lawyers named their new society after King Henry VIII; he removed a lot of land in Ireland from its owners, the Church, and leased part of it at Inns Quay (where the Four Courts are now located) to the new society. By the end of the 18th century, the government of the day decided that it needed a place to house the courts and so the society's land became the Four Courts. A new location was found for the society in 1800 – James Gandon, the architect of so many beautiful Georgian buildings in Dublin, was commissioned to design the present buildings on Constitution Hill. The building was to become the school of law, and the primary focus of the school is the training of barristers.

The School of Law is the oldest institution of professional legal education in Ireland. It has an international reputation, with a long list of eminent graduates including former presidents of Ireland and of other countries, taoisigh, politicians and, of course, judges and barristers in practice throughout the English-speaking world.

New Markets Area

The Victorian markets of Dublin were not being used to their full potential and have been redeveloped as part of the regeneration of the northwest of the city and Smithfields.

Autumn colour at the King's Inns

Old Jameson Distillery
(*See p36.*)

St Michan's Church
Built in 1686 on the site of a much older Viking church that dates from 1095. Some of the tower is from the original building and this is the oldest structure on the Northside of the Liffey. The leaders of the 1798 Rebellion were buried in the vaults and the church graveyard. The mummified bodies have been perfectly preserved there for over 200 years because of the rarefied and dry atmosphere – not for the squeamish, but fascinating viewing all the same. The second claim to fame is the very old organ, which allegedly was used by Handel to compose *The Messiah. Church St. Tel: (01) 872 4154. Open: mid-Mar–Oct Mon–Fri 10am–12.45pm & 2–4.30pm, Sat 10am–12.45pm; Nov–mid-Mar Mon–Fri 12.30–3pm, Sat 10am–12.45pm. Free admission.*

Temple Bar

Temple Bar is situated in one of the oldest parts of the city. The Vikings first built their longphort *here long ago when the area was actually under the waters of the River Liffey and the now underground River Poddle. After a period of considerable wealth and importance, especially during the 18th century, Temple Bar fell into neglect and disuse for most of the next two centuries.*

As you stroll around Temple Bar you are stepping in the footsteps of the Anglo-Irish aristocrat Sir William Temple who gave the area its name. With his family, he liked to promenade through the streets at the centre of one of Dublin's cultural heartlands.

But it is doubtful that the haughty Sir Temple, who was elected Trinity Provost in 1609, would approve of all of the nocturnal activity in Temple

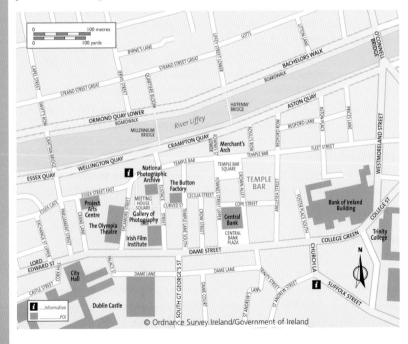

© Ordnance Survey Ireland/Government of Ireland

Temple Bar is the place to go for those wanting to sample Dublin's nightlife

Bar today. This is the place to go if you want to party all through the night, and you will need a strong constitution and stomach if you are going to last.

In the 1990s it was partly pedestrianised and redeveloped into the lively cultural centre it is today. The place is brimful with excellent pubs, cafés and restaurants. You can sample some of the current local arts scene in the four galleries in the area.

The Button Factory

Formerly the Temple Bar Music Centre, this venue has had a face-lift and now plays host to up-and-coming bands. It's also a club venue.

Curved St, Temple Bar.
Tel: (01) 670 9202. Fax: (01) 677 5566.
www.tbmc.ie

Irish Film Institute

With an arthouse cinema and bookshop, this venue is the hub of the Irish film industry. It holds various seminars and workshops throughout the year. The neon-floored entrance is particularly attractive and there is a café

for post-film discussions. The Dublin International Film Festival (*www.dubliniff.com*) is held in February. *6 Eustace St, Temple Bar.*
Tel: (01) 679 3477. www.irishfilm.ie

Meeting House Square

There used to be a Quaker hall here, and that is how the square got its name. In the summer there are outdoor screenings of films and various concerts of all types of music from classical to jazz. An organic food market is held in the square on Saturdays from 10am to 5pm.

Gallery of Photography

This is the only dedicated photography gallery in Dublin and it features contemporary work from Irish and foreign photographers.
Meeting House Square, Temple Bar.
Tel: (01) 671 4654.
www.galleryofphotography.ie. Open:
Tue–Sat 11am–6pm, Sun 1–6pm.
Closed: Mon. Free admission.

Temple Bar is known for its open-air markets

National Photographic Archive

This is the National Library's photographic collection, with over 300,000 photographs. Regular photographic exhibitions are held in the ground-floor foyer and you can ask to look through the extensive archive. They will also print pictures from the collection for you, for a fee.
Meeting House Square, Temple Bar.
Tel: (01) 603 0374. www.nli.ie.
Open: Mon–Fri 10am–5pm, Sat
10am–2pm. Free admission. Short walk
from city centre.

Project Arts Centre

A multidisciplinary arts centre, with art galleries and performance spaces. Holds various events throughout the year. Fostered the careers of Liam Neeson, Bono, Jim Sheridan, Neil Jordan and Gabriel Byrne.
39 Essex Street East, Temple Bar.
Tel: (01) 881 9613/14.
www.projectartscentre.ie

Temple Bar Square

This is the epicentre of Temple Bar and fills with people at lunchtime and in the early summer evenings who stop to listen to the buskers. The square was the site of one of the major fights in the 1916 Rising and it was here that the Telephone Exchange building was located. The failure to take control of the building was probably the most significant factor contributing to the early defeat of the Rising.

The north bank of the Liffey

Pub culture

Dublin is proud of its pubs and they have been the focus of social life for generations. Here you can gain an insight into the lives of the locals as everything is discussed, from politics through literature to sport. Conversation is still king in most pubs, although there has been an influx of jukeboxes and widescreen TVs showing 24-hour sports. However, you can still find a drinking hole where there is no noise except for conversation or perhaps a traditional band playing in the corner. This is the essence of Dublin pub life and there is no better place to be. Many of Dublin's literary giants spent much time in the pubs of Dublin and if you write your postcards over a pint of the black stuff, don't be too surprised if your friends and relatives compliment your literary eloquence when you get home. It will be, as they say in Dublin, 'the drink talking'. Music has always been an important part of the pub social scene in Dublin and you can listen to some excellent and authentic traditional music, rock or jazz if you find the right venue.

The traditional

The traditional Irish pub is Victorian in origin with wood panelling and stained glass and perhaps even a snug or two. These are the places where you are likely to encounter the ghost of some famous dead writer or poet or have a conversation with some budding literary talent who could be the next Joyce, Beckett or Yeats. There is no doubt when you listen to overheard conversations in Irish pubs that you will be inspired.

Palace Bar – a haunt of literary greats

The modern

Many popular modern pubs of myriad designs have sprung up all over the city of Dublin. There is a cluster of them in the Temple Bar area.

Dublin literary pub crawl

To get a flavour of the influence of the pub on the literary giants of Dublin literature, you could do worse than to take this award-winning guided tour run by two actors. The actors provide a humorous take on the drinking exploits of Dublin's writers and some extracts from their most famous works. You are encouraged to drink along the way and take in the atmosphere of the pubs, but you don't have to.
Meet at The Duke (upstairs), 9 Duke St. Tel: (01) 670 5602.
Email: info@dublinpubcrawl.com.
www.dublinpubcrawl.com. Summer (Apr–Nov), Mon–Sat 7.30pm, Sun noon & 7.30pm. Winter (Dec–Mar) Thur–Sat 7.30pm, Sun noon & 7.30pm. Nightly over the Christmas period. Busy in the summer and you may need to book.

A night out with the stags and hens

Dublin has become very popular with stag and hen nights (the party traditionally held before a wedding by the groom and bride respectively) from all parts of the UK. On some weekends in the summer there are up

A long-established tavern, the Auld Dubliner

to 500 different stag or hen nights in the city. Consequently, you may encounter a large crowd of over-boisterous drunken men or women wandering from pub to pub, especially around Temple Bar in the summertime. It is wise to steer clear of them and move to the other end of the bar when they come streaming into the pub to disrupt your quiet pint. They won't stay for long as they are probably on a pub crawl, visiting as many pubs as they can in the evening until their mobility is limited to crawling at some stage of the wee hours.

Trinity College

Trinity used to be the second most unpopular building in the city after Dublin Castle. From its foundation as a Protestant University by Queen Elizabeth I in 1592 until the 1970s, no Catholics were allowed to study in the University and many of its students were rich Protestants.

Protestant students did not have to qualify academically in any way to get in. In fact one of its most famous graduates, Samuel Beckett, had this to say about those who attended Trinity, which was also called Dublin University: 'Dublin University contains the cream of Ireland: rich and thick.' Such was the hatred of the place at the time that there are still a few elderly Dubliners who will not walk through the grounds on principle. Times have changed, however, and Trinity has now been embraced as part of the city.

The main gate of Trinity College at College Green is a popular meeting place for Dubliners. Two statues by sculptor John Foley stand guard at the entrance. The poet Oliver Goldsmith is on the right and political writer Edmund Burke on the left. As you pass through the entrance arch you enter Parliament Square with the bell tower (campanile) directly in front of you. It was built in 1853 and is nearly 30m (100ft) high. The red brick building in

Library Square is the Rubrics, which is the oldest remaining part of Trinity, dating to 1700. If you turn right from Parliament Square, you enter Fellows Square.

The Old Library, Trinity's main tourist attraction, is off Fellows Square.

The Berkeley Library, built by architect Paul Karolek, is also just off the square.

Beside this building and behind the sculpture is the attractive museum building. If you leave Trinity via the Nassau St exit, you might drop in and visit the Douglas Hyde Gallery.

The Old Library

Trinity's Old Library is the most important sight to see in the grounds of the University. It is over 60m (200ft) long and contains millions of tomes of famous published works. A copy of every book that is published in the UK is still donated to the library, despite the fact that Ireland has gained its independence.

The Book of Kells (AD 800)

This book is the top attraction in Dublin and one of the most beautiful books in the world. It is a Latin copy of the *Four Gospels* and it is most famous for its lavish decoration and depiction of saints, biblical characters and events. The book is Ireland's most treasured work of art. Most historians now agree that it was produced in St Colmcille's monastery on the Hebridean island of Iona off the coast of Scotland in the 8th century. After Viking raids, the monks fled from Iona to Ireland to set up a monastery at Kells near the Hill of Tara. The book was temporarily buried in the ground for safekeeping, but was recovered. At this time certain pages and the cover for the book were destroyed. It was moved to Trinity College in the 17th century. The other important ancient manuscripts in the library are *The Book of Armagh* (AD 807) and the even older *Book of Durrow* (AD 675).

The Long Room

This is the most attractive room in the building, containing 200,000 of the oldest books in the library. It houses the Proclamation read by Padraig Pearse in front of the GPO at the start of the Easter Rising in 1916. There is also an ancient harp that is said to have belonged to Brian Boru.

The Old Library, entrance on Fellows Square, Trinity College. Tel: (01) 896 2320. www.tcd.ie/Library/old-library. Open: Mon–Sat 9.30am–5pm, Sun (Oct–Apr) noon–4.30pm, Sun (May–Sept) 9.30am–4.30pm. Closed for 10 days over the Christmas period and New Year.

The bell tower (campanile)

Trinity College

A trip on the DART

The DART is the Dublin Area Rapid Transport electric train system (*see map, p27*). The journey from Greystones to the south into the city centre of Dublin has to rank as one of the most idyllic commutes into a capital city. Pick a good day to do this trip as the views are among the best in the country.

The journey here is described as the train leaves Greystones, but if you are staying in Dublin this will be the return journey. The tracks go right along the edge of the cliffs of Bray Head, and if you are brave enough you can look over the vertiginous drop to the waves crashing on the rocks below. You travel through a tunnel and the next stop is Bray's Daly Station. On your right you can see mural depictions of the use of the railway during the various eras of this stretch of the line. As you leave Bray and cross the River Dodder, you can see the harbour filled with swans on your right. Two stations later as you come into Killiney Station, you will see the Killiney Bay Court Hotel on the left-hand side. You are approaching the best part of your journey. The view spreads out in front of you and you can see the cliffs leading to Sorrento Terrace, one of the most expensive property areas in the country, and Dalkey Island behind it. Look behind you as Dublin Bay stretches majestically southwards to Bray Head and the Wicklow Mountains. You may see some surfers beneath you that look like seals in the waves below (there are some real seals in Dublin Bay as well), as this has become a popular surfing spot. After Dalkey, the scenery changes and is rather nondescript until you reach

Victorian bandstand in Dun Laoghaire

View south from Killiney

Dun Laoghaire station. Here you get a good view of the new marina and the famous piers. When you leave the West Pier behind, the views of the bay open up again and you can see Howth to the north. You may see some windsurfers in this area and some cormorants on the rocks. At Salthill you can see some of the Georgian houses on the left and on the right one of the Martello towers. This is a popular bathing spot. At Blackrock you can catch a glimpse of the old baths, and the sands will begin to come into view if the tide is out. On your left at Booterstown you will see the marshes that are an important reserve for seabirds that overwinter here each year. As you leave Booterstown, the views of Sandymount Strand at low tide will delight you. The reflections in the sandpools are beautiful even on the darkest of Dublin days and even the power station looks attractive. You may catch glimpses of the many oystercatchers flitting around the sands. Just before Sydney Parade you leave the views of the sweeping bay behind you and head towards the suburbia of the city. After Lansdowne Road station you will glimpse the stadium that is the home of the Irish rugby team. At Grand Canal Dock you will see some of the new Dublin architecture and some urban regeneration in progress. When you leave Tara St station you cross the River Liffey and get an interesting perspective of the magnificent Custom House building as the track sweeps around the side of it with the modern IFSC centre behind it. Get off at Connolly Station.

Dublin environs

Vagaries of the weather aside, Dublin must surely be the perfect city for a holiday. So much to see and do in the city, and when you are tired of pavements you can hop on the DART or a bus and in less than an hour be in a national park, walking wild unspoiled clifftops or wondering at megalithic architecture.

To the south of the city are the glorious Wicklow Mountains, with the Wicklow Way providing a route through the best of them; pretty seaside towns of Bray, Sandycove, Killiney and Dalkey; Glendalough with its haunting beauty; and grand houses to visit. To the north is Newgrange (a World Heritage site), some lovely old castles, the pretty little seaside town of Howth with its museum and cliff walk, the nature reserve of North Bull Island and much more.

A spectacular sky over Bray beach

SOUTH OF DUBLIN
Bray

Bray developed into a popular Victorian seaside resort when the Dublin to Dun Laoghaire railway was extended to the town in the 1850s. After a period during which it deteriorated into a rather rough holiday town with tacky amusement arcades and fish and chip shops, it has improved of late. The promenade makes for a pleasant stroll and an escape from the city, especially if you go to Bray out of season when you can avoid the summer crowds, and the beach is a lot cleaner than it once was. At the north end of the promenade there is a row of Georgian houses that form Martello Terrace. James Joyce lived at No 1. Joyce based the argument at the Christmas dinner table in *A Portrait of the Artist as a Young Man* at this location. One of Ireland's leading politicians now lives in the house. The Martello Tower was once owned by Bono of U2 fame.

Dublin environs

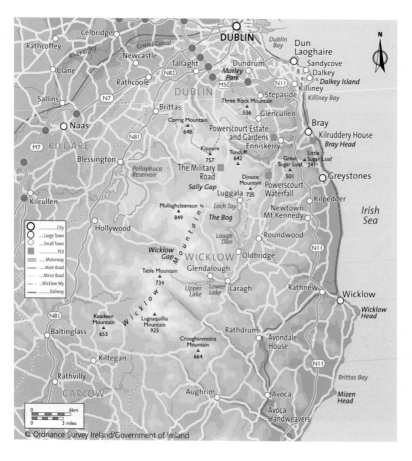

© Ordnance Survey Ireland/Government of Ireland

WICKLOW

For information about tourism in Wicklow
there is a tourist office in the Heritage Office
in front of the Royal Hotel in Bray.
*Bray Tourist Office, Old Courthouse, Lower
Main St, Bray. Tel: (01) 286 6796. Email:
infobray@eircom.net. Open: Jun–Aug Mon–Fri
9am–5pm & Sat (all year) 10am–3pm. Closed
at lunch 1–2pm; Sept–May Mon–Fri
9.30am–4.30pm. Bus 45, 45A, 84, 184. DART
from Dublin to Bray DART station.*

You can climb Bray Head in about an
hour from the railway station. This is a
steep climb through pretty woodland
and scrub to the cross at the top. You
will get a magnificent view of Bray,
northwards to the city, across to
Howth, southwards down to Wicklow
Head and in a westerly direction to the
mountains of Wicklow. On clear frosty
days in the winter, when the visibility
is excellent, you can even see as far
as Wales.

You can walk on to Greystones from
the top or make your way back to Bray
by heading down to the lower path
along the coast.

Kilruddery House

This has some pretty gardens and is
near Bray, but is difficult to access
without a car.
*Kilruddery. Tel: (01) 286 3405.
www.kilruddery.com. Open: May–Jun &
Sept daily 12.30–5pm. Admission charge.
Bus: 184 from Bray DART station.*

The railway line hugs the coast near Bray

A tranquil pond in front of Kilruddery House

Greystones

The end of the line as far as the DART is concerned. Greystones has changed considerably from the small fishing village that was here 30 years ago. It is now firmly in the commuter belt and expanding all the time. In spite of this it is a pleasant little place to spend half a day wandering around. There are two beaches in Greystones: the one near the railway station is a long sandy beach, and down by the small harbour the north beach is stony and stretches as far as the bottom of Bray Head. You can walk along the cliff face from Greystones into Bray in about 1^1/$_2$–2 hours.

Bus: 84, 184. DART from Dublin to Greystones DART station (about 30 mins).

Dalkey

The area of South County Dublin is one of the most affluent in the country. It is considered one of the most attractive places to live and the property prices reflect this.

This exclusive town in the suburbs of Dublin has had quite a chequered history. The area has been inhabited since ancient times and, according to the *Annals of the Four Masters*, in 'the year of the world 3501', there was a fort built here by a Milesian chief. In Viking times Danes fleeing from a battle in 942 used Dalkey Island as a refuge. The Vikings named the place Delginis, meaning 'Thorn Island' (still the Irish name for the town), which was subsequently changed to Dalkey.

In Norman times the town became a major harbour because the boats had become too large to go up the Liffey and so they deposited their cargo in Dalkey's Coliemore Harbour. At this time there were seven castles in the town. Two castles remain: the Goat Castle, which has been incorporated into the Town Hall, and Bullock Castle, which stands in ruin on the Dun Laoghaire Rd.

An eccentric group of locals started a tradition, the coronation of a King of Dalkey, in the 19th century. The full impressive title of the elected royal was 'King of Dalkey, Emperor of the Muglins, Prince of the Holy Island of Magee, Baron of Bulloch, Seigneur of Sandycove, Defender of the Faith and Respector of All Others, Elector of Lambay and Ireland's Eye, and Sovereign of the

Dalkey harbour

Most Illustrious Order of the Lobster and Periwinkle'.

Sorrento Terrace in Dalkey, which faces south towards Killiney and marks the southernmost point of Dublin Bay, is among the most sought-after property in the country. The view from this point can be stupendous in good weather.

Coliemore Harbour and Dalkey Island

You can catch a boat out to the island, which contains the remains of Neolithic man. The macabre climax of Samuel Beckett's great novel *Malone Dies* occurs when a male nurse takes a boatload of lunatics out on this very same trip. Lord Tullamore and his wife

FAMOUS LOCALS

In the past, novelist James Joyce and playwright George Bernard Shaw lived in Dalkey. The area has recently been dubbed 'Bel Eire' (playing on the word Eire for Ireland and Hollywood's exclusive Bel Air) because of the number of rich celebrities that live and have lived here. Among the more famous residents are a number of rock stars including three members of U2 (Bono, The Edge and Adam Clayton), Enya, Tina Turner, Van Morrison, Jim Kerr and Lisa Stansfield. Formula 1 racing drivers Michael Schumacher, Damon Hill and Eddie Irvine have all had houses here. Film director Neil Jordan and novelist Maeve Binchy also live here. Hollywood superstar Brad Pitt had a house here once.

once threw a party on Dalkey Island to celebrate the victory of King Billy at the Battle of the Boyne.
DART to Dalkey DART station.

Dalkey Village and Goat Castle

The village has a narrow main street with some exclusive shopping. The castle in Dalkey is called Goat Castle and it is one of the seven original tower houses of Dalkey, which date from 1429, when Dalkey was the main port of Dublin. There is a heritage centre dedicated to local history.
Dalkey Heritage Centre, Castle St.

Tel: (01) 285 8366. Fax: (01) 284 3141. www.dalkeycastle.com. Open: Mon–Fri 9.30am–5pm, Sat, Sun & Public Holidays 11am–5pm all year round. Closed Christmas and Easter. Admission charge.

Killiney

Hidden on the quiet roads around Killiney Hill are mansions that sometimes look more like castles and palaces than homes. You can climb the hill to enjoy some great views of Dublin Bay.
DART to Killiney DART station.

Dublin environs

Killiney Beach – a pleasant place for a morning stroll in the sunshine

Dun Laoghaire

In AD 480 King Laoghaire (pronounced Leary) is said to have founded a huge stone fort at the present site of Dun Laoghaire. This fort was in ruins and the present town was only a small fishing village when the construction of the pier began in the 1760s. The visit of King George IV in 1820 was probably the major impetus for the redevelopment of the town. The name was changed to Kingstown in his honour and the construction of the largest man-made harbour in the world, designed by John Rennie, was initiated. In 1834 the earliest suburban railway from Dublin to Dun Laoghaire was completed. The harbour complex was completed in 1842 and by then steamboat ferries were sailing here from Britain. The harbour took over from Howth as the major transport centre from Dublin to Britain, with steamboats going to both Holyhead and Liverpool. In 1918 the RMS *Leinster* was torpedoed by a German U-boat about 25km ($15^1/_2$ miles) from Kingstown and 500 lives were lost. After independence in 1922, the name of the town was changed back to Dun Laoghaire. During the 1960s car ferries were introduced.

The sun sets over Dun Laoghaire's famous harbour

The prom from Dun Loaghaire stretches as far as Sandycove

The East and West Piers are popular for walking, especially the East Pier, which on a weekend afternoon, no matter what the weather, can seem as crowded as George's St, the main street in Dun Laoghaire. The East Pier has an 1890s bandstand and an anemometer dating from the 1850s. This is a wind-speed measuring instrument and it was one of the world's first. There is an attractive lighthouse on the end of each pier and this is the best place to watch the sailing, especially on Wednesday evenings or at the weekends during the summer months. Sailing is popular in Dun Laoghaire and there are three yacht clubs. The Royal Irish Yacht Club opened in 1850 and was the first purpose-built yacht club in Ireland. The two others are the Royal St George and the National. The town of Dun Laoghaire has undergone a revamp, with the new pavilion shopping centre and entertainment complex being major additions.

The Martello tower in Sandycove featured in James Joyce's *Ulysses*

Sandycove

It is a very pleasant walk from Dun Laoghaire along the coastline to Sandycove, the home of the famous 'men only' bathing place and the location of the opening passage of James Joyce's *Ulysses*, as well as the start of the annual Bloomsday pilgrimage.

The Forty Foot Baths

The baths at Forty Foot are no longer 'men only' and you must wear bathing costumes when you swim there (at least a sign says so), but that was not always the case. The Forty Foot is not named after the depth of the water but rather after the soldiers of the Fortieth Regiment who were once stationed at a battery nearby and used to go swimming at this natural sea pool. Men have been bathing here in the nude for years, and if you have sensitive eyes be careful as any man may strip off in front of you and plunge into the ice-cold waters. Year-round swimming is a common practice at the Forty Foot for hardy souls.

The traditional swim on Christmas Day has become so popular that thousands of people come down to the Forty Foot and it can take 15–20 minutes to gain access. Even if the weather is fine and mild, the temperature of the water is freezing in the winter. It is not much warmer in the summer, and you have to be of strong constitution to swim in the Irish Sea. Those who swim here on Christmas Day work up quite an appetite for their Christmas dinner.

James Joyce Museum

Beside the Forty Foot is the granite tower and museum (more commonly called Joyce's tower) dedicated to Dublin's most famous writer, James Joyce. This is the traditional starting point of the annual Bloomsday pilgrimage. The museum contains many personal items including a piano and guitar, one of Joyce's trademark waistcoats, a tie and even his death mask, which seems to have captured the great man's last wry smile.

Joyce's tower, Sandycove, Co. Dublin. Tel & Fax: (01) 280 9265. Open: Apr–Aug Tue–Sat 10am–5pm (closed: 1–2pm), Sun 2–6pm; Sept–Mar by appointment. Admission charge.

Dublin environs

A James Joyce lookalike on Bloomsday

The Powerscourt Waterfall near Enniskerry

Enniskerry

Enniskerry is a small picturesque Georgian village that dates from the 1760s. Powerscourt House had need of a village for the sake of its tenants' convenience, and so the forest of Kilgarron was felled in order to accommodate the new Enniskerry village. The central landmark clock tower is a memorial to the Wingfield family, as Folliott Wingfield was Lord Powerscourt at the time.

Powerscourt Estate and Gardens

This is the foremost Anglo-Irish estate on the east coast of Ireland. The Italianate gardens, with their design and the backdrop of the Sugar Loaf Mountains, are probably the most extensive and exquisite in the whole country. Powerscourt House was designed in the 1730s by Richard Castle for Richard Wingfield, a member of the Irish Parliament and first Viscount of Powerscourt.

In 1974 a fire gutted the house and destroyed the restoration that was in progress. The Slazenger family, the current owners, have restored some of the house, but not all of it. The main attraction is the gardens; view the pebble mosaic below you, the Italian-style stairway leading down to the large pond, and the mountains behind you. Other highlights of the garden are the formal walled gardens and the **Japanese Garden**. The Wingfield family's **Pet Cemetery** is a curiosity, with an array of animal graves including those of their dogs, cats, horses and even their cows.

There are some exclusive shopping arcades, including an **Avoca Handweavers,** and an excellent restaurant in the house.
Tel: (01) 204 6000.
www.powerscourt.ie.
Open: daily 9.30am–5.30pm.
Gardens closed at dusk in winter.
Admission charge for the gardens.

Powerscourt Waterfall

This is the highest waterfall in Britain and Ireland at a height of 130m (426ft). After a period of rain, it is at its most spectacular. It is about a 5km (3-mile) walk from the estate to the waterfall, or you can drive around to the car park. There is a children's playground at the base of the waterfall – an idyllic spot for a picnic.
Open: Jan–Feb & Nov–Dec 10.30am–4pm; Mar–Apr & Sept–Oct 10.30am–5.30pm; May–Aug 9.30am–7pm.
Closed: two weeks before Christmas.
Admission charge for the waterfall.

Avoca

The picturesque town of Avoca is famous for its woollen mills and for the fact that the BBC TV series *Ballykissangel* was filmed in the town (*see p115*). The valley is one of the prettiest in Ireland and the confluence of the two rivers (the Avonmore and the Avonbeg), the Meeting of the Waters, is the focal point.

Dublin environs

Looking up towards Powerscourt House

Thomas Moore was so enchanted by the valley of Avoca that he was moved to write this verse: 'There is not in the wide world a valley so sweet/As that vale in whose bosom the bright waters meet.' In the springtime the valley is at its most beautiful, filled with cherry blossom. In the summer during the middle of the day it can get crowded as a lot of tour buses stop here.

In olden times there was a gold mine in the area and there are tiny slivers of gold in the river. The mine was closed as it was considered uneconomical and the

Creating textiles for Avoca's woollen mills on a several-hundred-year-old loom

gold dried up. You can always pan for gold, but you will need to be lucky to find enough to pay for your holiday. You will have more chance of winning the Irish Lottery (Lotto).

Avoca Handweavers

Avoca Handweavers have an old mill just outside the town of Avoca. This is the oldest hand-weaving mill in Ireland and you can see the weaving in action in the workshop. The weaving is carried out in small whitewashed buildings with red-painted doors and window frames. To some it might seem twee; to others it adds atmosphere and authenticity to the old way of producing garments. It is a good place to purchase the quality woollen produce that the Avoca company makes, but you can also get it in their shop in Dublin.

Avondale House

This was the former home of Charles Stewart Parnell, the 'uncrowned king of Ireland', who has a monument dedicated to him at the top of O'Connell St. Parnell was born in Avondale in 1842 and was one of the greatest politicians that Ireland has ever produced. His political career was destroyed by the scandal of an affair with Kitty O'Shea, the wife of another parliamentarian. The house was designed by John Wyatt, an English architect, and built at the end of the 18th century. The interior has been renovated in 19th-century style and filled with Parnell memorabilia. The State bought the house and the surrounding park in

BALLYKISSANGEL

This is the BBC TV series that made the village of Avoca famous and brought some prosperity to the area. The TV series has been discontinued but people still come from all over the world to see the street that was immortalised on TV screens. The story centres around a young English priest, Peter Clifford, who came to the small Irish village. He becomes enamoured (in his mind of course) with a beautiful Irish colleen. The story follows his struggles with his faith and the different culture of rural Ireland. At its height *Ballykissangel* had a huge cult following in Europe and America, where they still run repeats. There are many websites devoted to the series and even one *Fantasy Ballykissangel*, which continues the story in fantasy even though the series is long gone.

Getting to Avoca: Buses leave Busaras bus station on Store St in Dublin (Bus Eireann, tel: (01) 836 6111; www.buseireann.ie).

1904, and since then it has been an important site for forestry research. The first steps in Irish silviculture were made here and many exotic trees fill the park, which is especially scenic in the autumn when the leaves change colour.

Avondale House, Rathdrum. Open: Apr–Oct daily 11am–6pm. Last admission 5pm. Tel: (0404) 46111. Admission charge.

Avondale House is about 1.6km (1 mile) from the town of Rathdrum, and about a 20-minute walk from Rathdrum railway station. The Rosslare and Arklow trains, which leave from Connolly station, stop at Rathdrum railway station. Buses for Rathdrum leave Busaras bus station on Store St in Dublin (Bus Eireann, tel: (01) 836 6111; www.buseireann.ie).

NORTH OF DUBLIN
Clontarf

The suburb of Clontarf was the scene of one of Dublin's greatest battles and the home of the man who created one of the darkest characters in fiction.

The Battle of Clontarf

Brian Boru is the most famous of all the *Ard Rí* (High Kings) of Ireland. Born in AD 940 in Killaloe, County Clare, he was the second son of the Declassian clan. With his elder brother, Mahon, he won many battles against the Vikings. His brother was killed and, in 1002 at the Rock of Cashel in Tipperary, Brian Boru was crowned the High King of Ireland. After several attempts to seize Dublin he tried again

COUNT DRACULA

Bram Stoker created one of the best-known characters in fiction and probably the most famous in the horror genre. Born in Clontarf in 1847, he became an assistant to the famous actor Sir Henry Irving, who came to Dublin to do a show. Stoker went to England with Irving. His character, Count Dracula, was the first vampire to generate a cult following.
There have been countless film adaptations of *Dracula* and his adventures. The first was *Nosferatu* in German in 1922, but perhaps the most famous was Universal Studios' 1931 version, in which Bela Lugosi portrayed the evil Count.

Bram Stoker Dracula Experience, *West Wood Club, Clontarf Rd. Tel: (01) 805 7824. Open: Fri 4–10pm, Sat & Sun noon–10pm. Admission charge. DART from Dublin to Clontarf DART station.*

Clontarf Castle, now a hotel, is located at the site of one of Ireland's greatest battles

at Clontarf. On Good Friday in 1014, a ferocious battle started between Brian Boru and the *Ostmen* (Vikings) of Leinster. Clontarf was only a small fishing village at the time. His army defeated the Vikings, but Brian Boru and his son were killed during the fighting. The Vikings lost their power in Ireland and the country was free again until the Normans came. Brian Boru had made the ultimate sacrifice for his country. Ireland had lost its last High King, but since this victory against the Vikings Brian Boru has been considered a national hero and symbol of Irish victories over foreign invaders. His body was buried with great pomp and ceremony at Armagh.

Brian Boru had many wives and is considered to be the original father of the O'Brien clan.

Casino at Marino

This building is an architectural masterpiece and the most important

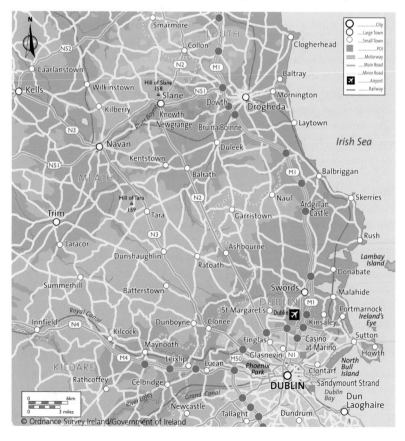

© Ordnance Survey Ireland/Government of Ireland

Palladian neoclassical building in Ireland. Lord Charlemont commissioned the building as a garden pavilion in his Marino Estate, which was unfortunately destroyed in the 1920s. The architect of the casino was Sir William Chambers and it was completed in the mid-1770s.

In 1930 it became government property and has recently been renovated. There are 16 finely decorated rooms. The chimneys in the building are sculpted urns and the drains are disguised as columns. Four lions stand guard at each of the corners. *Off the Malahide Rd. Tel: (01) 833 1618. www.heritageireland.ie. Open: Nov–Mar Sat & Sun noon–4pm; Apr Sat & Sun noon–5pm; May & Oct daily 10am–5pm; Jun–Sept daily 10am–6pm. Last admission 45 minutes before closing. Guided tours only. Admission charge. Bus: 20A, 20B, 27, 27B, 42, 42C.*

Howth

Howth is a pretty little town with steep, narrow cobbled streets and a wide harbour. The Vikings named the town Howth (*Hoved* in the Viking tongue means 'head') and it is one of the few place names of Viking origin left in the Dublin area. It remains a working fishing port and is a popular sailing location with a busy marina.

Howth is very close to the island of Lambay, which was one of the first places that the Vikings attacked when they came to Ireland. Howth Head is the northernmost point of Dublin Bay.

Howth Harbour is a haven for sailing craft

The most famous person to visit Howth was King George IV in 1820. Unfortunately, his arrival was more ignominious than ceremonious, as he struggled off the royal yacht drunk. He left one of his footprints on the pier. Howth was the original Packet Station before Kingstown (now Dun Laoghaire) took over after the visit of George IV in 1820. The author and Irish nationalist Robert Erskine Childers smuggled German guns into the harbour to arm the Nationalist Irish Volunteers on his yacht, *The Asgard*.

The town has a large, active working harbour. In the early morning the brightly coloured fishing boats bring in their catch of fish that will supply Dublin's restaurants. In the summertime the bay fills up with sails, as the local club is one of the largest yacht clubs in the city. Many of the yachts are the attractive wooden local design, the Howth 17s. The stroll out to the lighthouse on the end of the harbour is a favourite pastime at all times of the year, especially during the weekends.

Howth Castle

Howth Castle was bequeathed to the Norman noble Sir Almeric Tristram in 1177. He was involved in the battle against the Vikings with Baron John DeCoucry. Tristram claimed to be a descendant of Sir Tristram, one of the legendary Knights of the Round Table of King Arthur. After he won a battle with the divine help of St Lawrence, he decided to change the family name to St Lawrence. The castle has been the seat of the St Lawrence family since then.

The original motte Norman castle was rebuilt in 1564 and has had various alterations by leading architects, including British architect Sir Edwin Lutyens in 1910. The demesne and gardens are justly renowned for their beauty, particularly in spring and early summer when the rhododendrons are in flower.

As with practically every castle in Ireland, there is a ghostly story associated with Howth Castle. The story is of the pirate Grace O'Malley (or Granuaile) who lived on the west coast of Ireland. She had been to visit the Queen in England and on her way back she called into Howth Castle, which was the main port for Dublin at the time. She was refused entry and hospitality. This so infuriated the pirate queen that she stormed off with one of the heirs of the house and her ransom was for the door of the castle to be unlocked and left open for the O'Malley clan.

Even now the door of the castle is left ajar and an extra place is set in case Granuaile or one of her clan returns. The ghost of the pirate queen may be seen in these parts, and, if you bump into her, it is best to treat her with kindness and respect.

The castle is not open to the public but you can visit the castle grounds.

National Transport Museum

In the grounds of Howth Castle there is a museum of Dublin's transport run by a group of volunteers. There are exhibits of some early forms of transport and various memorabilia, including photographs.

Tel: (01) 847 5623.

(*Cont. on p122*)

Howth Castle

Walk: Howth Head

This walk starts from Howth DART station, which is about a 45-minute journey on the DART from the centre of Dublin. There are spectacular views on a clear day up the coast to the Mourne Mountains and out across Howth Head to the south. Some parts of the cliff are dangerous and you need to have proper walking shoes.

Allow at least 3 hours.

1 The Bloody Stream Pub

This pub has a rather gory name but some excellent food. It is named after a particularly hard battle fought at the Evora Bridge on this spot. In 1177 the Norman Baron John DeCourcy had a ferocious battle with the Vikings in Howth. So much blood was let that it formed a stream that flowed in the spot where this pub is now located. The stream kept flooding the pub and so they decided to give the pub its name to placate the ghosts of those who fought in the battle and lost their lives.
Walk towards the harbour.

2 Howth Harbour

An active harbour with a lighthouse and brightly coloured fishing boats.
Follow the road to the right at the entrance to the harbour. It goes right round to the start of the walk proper.

3 Martello tower

You have to be careful not to miss the tower because it is almost behind and above you. It makes an appearance in Joyce's *Ulysses* as the site of the first date of Leopold Bloom and his unfaithful wife Molly. It currently houses a small radio museum.

4 Ireland's Eye

About 1.6km (1 mile) offshore, Ireland's Eye island is now a bird sanctuary. On the island are the ruins of an old chapel, the successor of one built in the 7th century by the sons of St Nessan. There is also one of the Martello towers that dot the coastline and were erected to provide protection against an invasion by Napoleon that never actually materialised. In the summer you can take a boat out to the island from the harbour. There is a large colony of puffins on the island. You can see Lambay Island in the distance beyond Ireland's Eye.

5 Howth's Nose

There is some spectacular clifftop scenery around the Nose of Howth, and just beyond the Nose was the site of a marine disaster in 1853, when the steamship *Queen Victoria* ran aground on Casana Rock.

6 Baily Lighthouse

The Baily is an unusual cottage-type lighthouse. There has been some form of light on the head for over 300 years. The first lighthouse was built here in 1668 and the current one dates from 1790. Note that it is not open to the public. The Baily Lighthouse is on a peninsula and legend has it that this is the site of some buried treasure. From the promontory on clear days you get fantastic views of the Wicklow coastline and mountains, and even as far as the Welsh mountains across the sea.

7 Aideen's Grave

At the foot of Carrickmore Hill are the remains of a cromlech that, according to legend, was the burial place of Aideen, a Celtic princess, in AD 248. The walk follows on around the cliff until you reach Sutton Strand and then to the main road, which heads into Sutton itself.

From here you can catch a DART back into town.

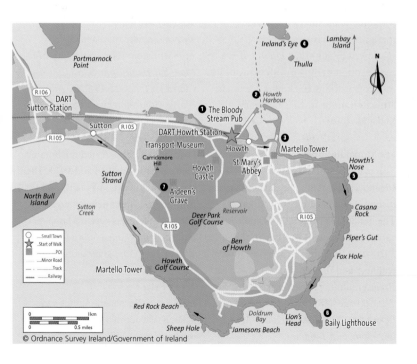

© Ordnance Survey Ireland/Government of Ireland

www.nationaltransportmuseum.org.
Open: Jun–Aug Mon–Sat 10am–5pm;
Sept–May Sat, Sun & Public Holidays
2–5pm; 26 Dec–1 Jan 2–5pm.
Admission charge.

St Mary's Abbey

The ruins of the old abbey provide one
of the best views of the harbour, with
Ireland's Eye beyond. The abbey was
founded by King Sitric (he also
founded Christ Church in the city) in
1042. Most of the ruins are from the
15th and 16th centuries. The tomb of
Lord Howth is in the grounds.
Abbey St. Free admission.

Malahide

Malahide is a pleasant town and
marina, but it has almost been
swallowed by suburban Dublin. It is a
major commuter town with many of its
residents working in Dublin. The main
attraction in the town is the huge
Malahide Castle.

Fry Model Railway

This is a huge model railway of
Ireland's rail system. For rail enthusiasts
it should be top of the tour itinerary.
The handmade train models are from a
collection originally built up in the
1920s and 1930s by Cyril Fry, a railway
engineer and draughtsman.
In the grounds of Malahide Castle.
Tel: (01) 846 3779. www.visitdublin.com.
Open: Apr–Sept Tue–Sat 10am–1pm
& 2–5pm, Sun 1–6pm.
Admission charge.

Malahide Castle

Prince John first donated Malahide
Castle to Robert Talbot in 1185. The
Talbots lived here continuously until
1975, apart from a brief period when
Oliver Cromwell temporarily evicted
them. It was the longest occupation of
any house in Ireland by a single family.
The seventh Baron died in 1973 after
the family had been in the house 800
years. It is said that 14 Talbot cousins
had breakfasted here before they went
off to be killed at the Battle of the
Boyne in 1690. The castle has the only
surviving original medieval great hall,
which dates from the 15th century and
houses an impressive collection of
family portraits.
Tel: (01) 846 2184.
www.malahidecastle.com. Open:
Apr–Sept daily 10am–5pm; Oct–Mar
Mon–Sat 10am–5pm, Sun 11am–5pm.
Closed for tours: 12.45–2pm. Admission
charge. Admission by tour only.

Talbot Botanic Gardens

Lord Milo Talbot created the botanic
gardens between 1948 and 1973. There
are over 500 species of plants and trees
from the southern hemisphere.
Tel: (01) 846 2456. Open: May–Sept
daily 2–5pm. Guided tour on
Wed at 2pm. Admission charge.

Tara's Palace

Inspired by Sir Neville Wilkinson's
Titania's Palace of 1907, this toy
museum has a collection of dolls'
houses and small replicas of three

18th-century mansions – Leinster House, Castletown House and Carlton House.

Malahide Castle Demesne.
Tel: (01) 846 3779. www.taraspalace.ie.
Open: Apr–Sept Tue–Sat 10am–1pm &
2–5pm, Sun & Public Holidays 1–6pm.
Admission charge.

Skerries

The town of Skerries is 30km (18½ miles) north of Dublin city centre. A small fishing town with good shops and restaurants, it also has a long sandy beach. *Train to Skerries Station and then a 5-minute walk or catch bus No 33 from Eden Quay.*

The reflected majesty of Malahide Castle

Dublin environs

The Skerries Mills

This 16th-century mill complex contains a water mill and two windmills. There used to be a bakery here in the 1840s. All three mills are in working order and you can go on a guided tour.

Tel: (01) 849 5208.
www.skerriesmills.org. Open: daily 10am–5.30pm. Closed: 20 Dec–1 Jan, Good Friday. Admission charge.

Balbriggan

Balbriggan is a coastal town about 32km (20 miles) north of Dublin with a pleasant beach and a Martello tower. According to legend, St Patrick baptised his successor, St Benignus, here in AD 436, in the River Delfin. King William of Orange set up camp in Balbriggan after winning the Battle of the Boyne in 1690.

Train to Balbriggan or bus 33 from Eden Quay. By car: signposted off the N1.

Ardgillan Castle

This castle was built in 1738 by Robert Taylor and set in 80 hectares (194 acres) of rolling pastureland, mixed woodlands and garden. Ardgillan means 'high woodland'. It has a dramatic setting on a piece of elevated coastline between Balbriggan and Skerries. It houses the permanent exhibition of 17th-century 'Down Survey' maps of Ireland. The garden contains a fine Victorian conservatory and a fragrant rose garden which is spectacular when the flowers are in bloom.

Tel: (01) 849 2212.
Open: Apr–Sept Tue–Sun & Public Holidays 11am–6pm; Oct–mid-Dec & Feb–Mar Wed–Sun & Public Holidays 11am–6pm; mid-Dec–Jan Sun only 2–4pm. Park & gardens open all year 10am–6pm. Admission charge. Bus 33 from Eden Quay. Ardgillan is signposted from the N1.

Slane

The church at Slane on the hill above Slane village marks an important spot in the legend of St Patrick and is a holy site for Irish Catholics. It has been called the 'Cradle of Irish Christianity'.

Yet Patrick may not have been there at all. In the 7th century the O'Neills controlled Tara and they wanted their king to be promoted to High King, so they created a fictitious association with St Patrick. According to legend, Patrick knew that he would have to gain the support of King Laoghaire, the High King of Tara, in order to establish the freedom to take his message throughout Ireland.

On Easter Sunday, 25 March AD 433, the traditional start of spring, Patrick built a paschal fire on the Hill of Slane in front of the King's domain, an act which was strictly forbidden. On seeing this, King Laoghaire was infuriated and went out to see the group who had challenged his command. However, he was so taken with St Patrick that he let him have the freedom to preach his message. St Patrick allegedly consecrated the church, the ruins of

One of the Skerries mills

which are still on the hill, and he stayed here for a while, converting many of the people in the surrounding area to Christianity. The first Bishop of Slane, St Erc, built the first monastery on the Hill of Slane some time in the 5th century.

Slane Castle

This Norman-built castle was bought by the Conyninghams after the Battle of the Boyne and has remained in the family ever since. The current owner, Lord Mountcharles, is a rock fan and has made use of the natural amphitheatre in the grounds, making it one of Ireland's premier music venues. U2, the Rolling Stones, Bob Dylan, David Bowie, Neil Young, Queen and Bruce Springsteen have all played here. U2 also recorded their album *The Unforgettable Fire* in the castle.
Slane. Tel: (041) 988 4400.
www.slanecastle.ie. Tours: Jun–Aug,
Sun–Thur noon–5pm.
Admission charge.

Ruins of the abbey at the Hill of Slane

Trim Castle

Trim Castle

The largest Anglo-Norman castle still standing in Ireland was constructed in 1173 for the Norman Lord Hugh DeLacy. The square keep, which is one of the only two remaining Norman keeps in Ireland, was not, however, completed until about 1200. King John visited Trim in 1210 and it is sometimes called King John's Castle, although DeLacy would not let him in the gate and he had to camp outside on the banks of the Boyne.

In medieval times Trim Castle marked the edge of the Pale. This was the patch of land that circled and included Dublin under Anglo-Norman control. Outside the Pale, the wild Irish were out of control. To go beyond the Pale, the Normans would have to risk entering a hostile world of 'Celtic savages'. In 1649 the castle came under the control of Cromwell and it has remained unoccupied since. The film *Braveheart*, starring Mel Gibson, used Trim Castle as a backdrop for a number of scenes. *Trim. Tel: (046) 943 8619. Open: Easter–Sept daily 10am–6pm; Oct daily 9.30am–5.30pm; Nov–Apr Sat & Sun 10am–5pm. Admission charge.*

Drogheda

Founded by the Vikings in AD 911 between two hills, Drogheda became an extremely important town during Norman times. They formed settlements on either side of the river and gave the port on the River Boyne its name, which comes from the Irish *Droichead Atha* ('Bridge of the Ford' in English).

However, it was the Normans who built up the fortifications of the town and established it as one of the most important towns in all of Ireland. A Norman fort (motte) on Millmount Hill still dominates the town, and this is where you get the best views of the environs. There is still an atmospheric medieval feel to the town, with narrow cobbled streets, although you should pick a bright day to visit, as it can seem a little dour and grey on a day with overcast skies. The impressive medieval Courthouse building (or *Tholsel*, as the Vikings called it) is still intact and two medieval gates also remain standing – St Lawrence Gate and the Butter Gate.

Drogheda was the location of one of the greatest atrocities in Ireland's history. It was here that the reviled Oliver Cromwell carried out one of his most ignominious acts. In 1649 he attacked the town, and though the locals put up a fierce resistance it was to no avail. Cromwell's army killed up to 3,000 of the town's inhabitants and many of the surviving women and children were sold off as slaves to the West Indies. The town was also on the losing side during the Battle of the Boyne. Since then it has only been a shadow of its former glory, and the decline in the local and traditional milling and brewing industries has not helped.

Millmount Museum

High on the hill of the same name is a museum dedicated to the history of the town, but there is little about Cromwell. There is a restored Martello tower and you can get magnificent views of the surroundings on a clear day.
Millmount Square. Tel: (041) 983 3097. www.millmount.net. Open: Mon–Sat 9.30am–5.30pm, Sun & Public Holidays 2–5pm. Admission charge.

St Peter's Church

There are two churches with the same name, but although the Protestant one (on Magdalene St) is older and has some interesting old gravestones, the Catholic one has one great treasure even if it seems a bit macabre. It is the home of the head of St Oliver Plunkett, which has been preserved and is on display behind glass. St Oliver was the Archbishop of Armagh and the Primate of Ireland. In 1672, when the Earl of Essex was made Viceroy of Ireland, there was a ban on practising Catholicism. St Oliver continued to wander around the country in civilian clothes converting people to Catholicism. He was falsely accused of the Popish Plot, which aimed at the murder of King Charles II, the massacre

of thousands of Protestants and establishing Roman Catholicism as the dominant religion again in Ireland. He was imprisoned in Dublin Castle and put on trial. He could not be found guilty in Ireland even though it was a Protestant jury, so his trial was moved to London. Here he was sentenced to death and to be hung, drawn and quartered. Even though the Earl of Essex pleaded at the last minute with King Charles II for clemency, St Oliver was martyred in 1681. He was made a saint after some miracles were performed in his name in Spain.
St Peter's Catholic Church, West St.

Tel: (041) 983 8239.
www.saintpetersdrogheda.ie

Drogheda is on the M1 motorway, which is the main route between Dublin and Belfast.
Buses for Drogheda leave from Busaras bus station in Dublin on an hourly basis during the day (Bus Eireann, tel: (01) 836 6111; www.buseireann.ie). Drogheda bus station is just south of the river on New St. Trains for Drogheda leave from Connolly station. Drogheda railway station is also south of the river and to the east of the town. It is just off the Dublin Rd.

Dublin environs

St Peter's Roman Catholic Church, Drogheda

Getting away from it all

The county of Wicklow, perhaps one of the most stereotypically 'emerald' of all Ireland's counties, with spectacular mountain scenery, the hidden valleys of Glendalough and its ancient pilgrimage history, or the Valley of the Boyne with its Neolithic settlement: beyond the immediate delights of the city centre and its suburbs lie many other attractions well worth a day trip away from the capital.

GLENDALOUGH

The name Glendalough comes from *Gleann dá locha* ('Valley of the two lakes'). This beautiful valley with steep-sided hills is extremely picturesque and is one of the finest in Ireland. The presence of the ancient monastic site with the round tower adds just that extra little bit of magic and mystique to the place.

Although there is evidence of pre-Christian habitation in Glendalough, not much is known about the valley until St Kevin arrived.

St Kevin was born in about AD 498 and allegedly died 120 years later in AD 618. Born into a wealthy family, St Coemgen (St Kevin) abandoned his life of privilege and went to study under the British monk St Petroc. He then decided to live a reclusive life in a small cave in the valley at Glendalough. He spent his life close to nature and in contemplation and prayer. He undertook severe Lenten penance and used to lie for days on a

cold slab of rock and stand up to his waist in the freezing waters of the lakes for hours each day. His reputation as a holy man spread, and people came to him to receive teaching. St Kevin was more fond of animals than of people and it is reported he pushed someone who came to visit him over a cliff. But his love of animals was famous and, according to legend, when a blackbird laid an egg on his hand he kept it outstretched until the egg hatched. At the end of the 6th century, St Kevin founded a monastery at Glendalough at the confluence of two small streams, and by the 9th century it was one of the most important sites of the early Celtic Christian church.

St Laurence O'Toole is the second saint associated with Glendalough, with St Saviour's Church in Glendalough dedicated to him. He was also born, as St Kevin was, of a rich family, the Leinster Chieftains, and was Abbot of Glendalough for nine years. He then became Archbishop of Dublin and was involved in the founding of the present-day stone version of Christ Church Cathedral with Strongbow. Although he was Archbishop of Dublin, St Laurence came to Glendalough every year for a 40-day retreat. St Laurence died in 1180 in Normandy in France.

From the original monastery a monastic village and university were established. It grew to be an important international centre of religious learning. Hundreds of students attended the university for ecclesiastical and secular studies. The monastery here flourished until the early 1200s, but it declined thereafter for a period and was not inhabited. In 1214 King John amalgamated the Glendalough Diocese with the Dublin Diocese because Glendalough had become dangerous to visit. According to the Archbishop of Tuam it was no longer a Christian place but 'A den of

Round tower, Glendalough

Kevin's cell and Upper Lake, Glendalough

thieves and a pit of robbers. More murders are committed in that valley than in any other part of Ireland'. Although after this period it lost its former importance it still continued as a monastic settlement. The end of monasticism was marked by an attack by English troops in 1398, when they razed the monastic village to the ground and left it in ruins. It was still an important place of pilgrimage until the 1860s, and on St Kevin's Day in June fairs or 'pattern days' were held here. Seven pilgrimages to Glendalough were, at this stage, considered to be equivalent to one pilgrimage to Rome. The pilgrimages, especially on the pattern days, were, however, only partly religious, as they were rather raucous parties and more by way of hooley than acts of devotion. It was the rowdiness and drunkenness at these events that eventually led the Catholic Church to put a ban on pilgrimages to Glendalough.

To reach Glendalough: Bus: St Kevin's bus service runs from Dublin to Glendalough. Leaves at 11.30am and 6pm from outside the Mansion House on

Dawson St (times may vary for the later bus in Jul and Aug). Tel: (01) 281 8119. www.glendaloughbus.com

Glendalough Visitors' Centre

The Visitors' Centre at Glendalough village provides information on the monastic settlement founded by St Kevin and also on the history of the valley, the archaeology and the local wildlife.

Tel: (0404) 45325. Open: mid-Oct–mid-Mar 9.30am–5pm; mid-Mar–mid-Oct 9.30am–6pm. Admission charge.

The monastic village

The great round tower or bell tower dominates the site and it is 33m (109ft) high and 16m (53ft) in circumference round the base. It was used to defend the village against Viking attack in the 9th century. The large ancient Celtic cross, which dates from the 9th or 10th century, is called the wishing cross. If you can wrap your arms around it so that your hands meet on either side, your wish will be granted. Also in the grounds is the unusual St Kevin's Church, or St Kevin's Kitchen, as it has been named. This nave and chancel church dates from the 11th century and has a small round tower above the doorway. There are some other remains from the time of St Kevin dotted around the valley. As a pilgrimage site, Glendalough was at one stage considered more important than Rome. The monastery here flourished until the early 1200s, but it declined when the Glendalough diocese joined up with Dublin.

The two lakes

The lakes of the valley are called Upper and Lower Lake, but the Lower Lake was originally called Loch Peist or 'lake of the water monster'. As in Scotland, there were rumoured to be water monsters that inhabited the deep mountain lakes of Ireland. St Kevin got on particularly well with the water monster, and the saint pacified its aggressive nature. The water monsters were associated with pagan gods and it was quite common for them to be destroyed by Christian saints, or so the Christian clergy at the time would have you believe. Of the two lakes, the Upper Lake is the more beautiful, and the light on the sides of the valley helps you understand why St Kevin decided to escape from it all and set up home here.

The pilgrimage routes

There are so many walks from Glendalough that they would merit a book in themselves. The most celebrated are the ancient pilgrimage routes that pass through the valley. The most famous is St Kevin's Road, which comes from the west over the Wicklow Gap from the Irish Hollywood. The Green Road pilgrimage way, which forms part of the Wicklow Way, runs through the monastic village and you will travel along it when you walk from the monastery to the lakes of Glendalough.

In the spirit of St Kevin, there are small *cillins* or basic accommodation units where you can spend some time in peaceful reflection, much as St Kevin would have done all those years ago. There is no pressure to be involved in any religious activities if you do not wish to, but they are available.

Glendalough 2000, St Kevin's Parish, Glendalough, Co. Wicklow.
Tel: (0404) 45777.
Email: glendalough2000@eircom.net

BEACHES

One on the Northside (North Bull Island) and the other on the Southside (Sandymount Strand), these two large beaches are perfect places for you to get away from the city, relax or go for a long walk.

North Bull Island

The Bull, as the locals call it, is a large sand island that has become an important nature reserve because many species of wading birds come here to overwinter. Some of the species to look out for in winter are brent geese, redshanks and bar-tailed godwits. In summer you will hear skylarks. There are also some protected rare orchids that flower in the summer.

The Bull is an artificial island created in the 1820s after the construction of the North Bull Wall. The engineer for the project was a certain Captain Bligh of mutiny on HMS *Bounty* fame. At low tide you can drive on the beach or walk out on the North Bull Wall to the lighthouse. The tide moves quite quickly on the way in so do not go too far from your car lest the salt water seeps into it. There is a Visitor Centre, and one of Ireland's finest golf courses, Royal Dublin, is also on Bull Island.

The Visitor Centre is open daily 10am–4.30pm. Free admission.
Bus: 30, 31.

Sandymount Strand

About 3km (2 miles) south of Dublin, Sandymount Strand, an expanse of shallow tidal flats, is a popular place for city dwellers to come and relax in the evening, taking a stroll on the sands following the boardwalk which skirts along the side of the road.

Alternatively, you can hike out on the South Wall to view the lighthouse and the passing ferries from Dublin port, which seem to come within touching distance. Some people fly kites on Sandymount Strand when the wind blows. The Strand features in the Bloomsday of Stephen Dedalus in *Ulysses*, who is making his way back to Dalkey from Dublin. He utters the words 'Am I walking into eternity along Sandymount Strand?'

The tide goes so far out that the tidal pools and the sky do often seem to blend into infinity and you can see why Dedalus felt the way he did. With the sun setting on Dun Laoghaire in the distance, there is no more beautiful place so close to the city.

Dollymount Strand, North Bull Island

VALLEY OF THE BOYNE

The Boyne Valley just north of Dublin is one of the earliest inhabited places in Ireland and has had a considerable influence on Irish history through the ages. The fertile valley attracted Neolithic farmers to the area, and at Brú na Boinne their prehistoric passage tombs stand testament to a civilisation older than the ones that constructed Stonehenge or even the Pyramids. There is plenty to see on a day trip, or perhaps you will be able to stay a few days.

The Boyne

The historic Battle of the Boyne was fought on the banks of the Boyne River in 1690. It was between the armies of Protestant Prince William of Orange and Catholic King James II. The year before, William had deposed James as King of England.

On 12 July the most famous battle in Irish history began and the Catholics were defeated. Ulster Unionists in the North of Ireland celebrate the victory on 12 July each year with parades in honour of William of Orange (they call him King Billy). The battle represented the climax of a century of bloody conflict in Ireland over land and religion, and it marked the beginning of a dark era for Irish Catholics. The sites of the Battle of the Boyne are marked along the side of the road.

Brú na Boinne

Brú na Boinne translates to 'Bend in the Boyne' and it is the site of Ireland's most important archaeological

The underground tombs at Newgrange

The site of the Battle of the Boyne

heritage – the ancient passage tombs dating from 2200 BC. The whole area has been designated a World Heritage Site by UNESCO. These prehistoric passage tombs built on the sides of the Boyne are evidence of Ireland's earliest farming communities. They are called passage tombs because there is an underground passage to the burial chamber. The passage tomb is covered by a distinctive mound of earth and stone, called a 'cairn'. They are visible from quite a long way off. There are three major archaeological sites in the area: Newgrange, Dowth and Knowth (*see p141*).

Brú na Boinne Visitor Centre

This modern building was constructed in the mid-1990s despite the controversy associated with building an interpretation centre so near to the ancient sites. But, that said, it is quite attractive from an architectural perspective. It has been built into the surrounding landscape so that it does not stand out too much. There are displays about the Neolithic sites in the Boyne Valley and a replica of the Newgrange site. This is how you access the ancient sites of Newgrange and Knowth.

Donore. Tel: (041) 988 0300. Newgrange open all year; Knowth open daily Feb–Apr

9.30am–5.30pm; May 9am–6.30pm; Jun–mid-Sept 9am–7pm; mid-Sept–end Sept 9am–6.30pm; Oct 9.30am–5.30pm; Nov–Feb 9.30am–5pm. A tour of the centre, Newgrange and Knowth will take 3 hours. Admission charge.

Hill of Tara

The Hill of Tara has been a place of mystical importance since early times. The passage tomb, the Mound of Hostages, dates from 2500 BC, around the same time as the ancient tombs of Brú na Boinne. But it is around 1000 BC that Tara really came to prominence as the seat of the *Ard Rí* ('High Kings of Ireland'), who were part High King and part Celtic pagan priests or druids. Tara was the spiritual centre of pagan and Celtic Ireland and the cult of the sun deity was practised here.

The remains of the Iron Age fort at the Hill of Tara date from this time.

Mound of Hostages, Hill of Tara

THE *TUATHA DÉ DANAAN*

According to legend, the first settlers in the area of the Hill of Tara were the ancient mythical race called the *Tuatha dé Danaan*, who hailed from Greece. They were the people of Danu and came to Ireland in a mystical mist. They were fierce warriors and sorcerers and they defeated their predecessors, the giant *Firbolgs*, with ease and banished them to the West of Ireland. It was the *Tuatha dé Danaan* who brought the magic stone, *Lía Fáil*, to Tara. They ruled Ireland until they were defeated by the Milesians from Spain. The descendants of the Milesians are thought to make up a considerable proportion of the Irish Gaels today. After their defeat, the *Tuatha dé Danaan*, a magical race, decided to live underground. They went into their otherworld (a supernatural realm) via a number of sites or portals, including the ancient burial tomb at Newgrange. According to legend they now occupy the *sidhe* ('fairy rings') around the country. You will see these mounds of earth marked by a circle of trees, as farmers believe it is bad luck to dig up the earth near them. One of the *Tuatha dé Danaan* and a queen of Ireland was Eire, who gave the country its name.

The ruins of the two main *raths* ('ring forts') still visible are *Tech Cormac* ('Cormac's House') and the Rath of Kings. The standing stone in Cormac's House is the *Lía Fáil* ('Magical Destiny Stone') with its fertility symbol. The ancient mythical race, the *Tuatha dé Danaan*, is said to have brought the magic stone to Tara. It is thought that it was the inauguration stone for the *Ard Rí* and it would let out a shout of approval in favour of the chosen High King. At Tara there is an alignment with the sun and moon that underlines the importance of the sun in the fertility of kinship that was part of the beliefs of the ancient Irish. The Chamber of the Mound of Hostages at Tara is lit by the full moon in August (date of the ancient Lughnasa harvest festival), and the rising sun at the festival of Samhain ('summer's end') on 1 November and Imbolg (the spring festival) in February.

Five great ancient roads radiated from Tara, including the *Slighe Cualann*, which went down to Wicklow via the site of the Ford of Hurdles that gave Dublin its Irish name, *Baile Atha Cliath*. Although there were thousands of years of activity, the construction of Tara is attributable to one legendary Iron Age King, Cormac Mac Airt. At the time of Cormac, according to archaeologists on the site, there would have been a series of wooden buildings enclosed in a large oval-shaped enclosure that was on top of a hill. The statue of St Patrick at the Hill of Tara is a statement of the arrival of Christianity and was deliberately placed on the spot to downplay the pagan associations of the hill. Early Christian historians realised the importance of Tara, and it was here that they placed the greatest confrontation of St Patrick and the new Christian religion, and the druids of the old religion. St Patrick may not have been here at all, but the historians wanted him to be. In 1843 Daniel O'Connell, recognising the significance of Tara and its importance in the eyes of the Irish people, held one of his famous monster rallies here to

St Patrick called upon his faith to defeat the druids at Tara

demonstrate against the way Irish Catholics were treated by their Protestant rulers. At the time of writing, and despite ongoing protests from campaigners who fear that it jeopardises Tara, a new motorway (the M3) that will pass very close to the site is under construction.

Knowth and Dowth

At Knowth there are two passages to different burial tombs in the main burial cairn, and up to 17 satellite cairns around the area. On the hill at Knowth there was an early Christian village and, even later, a Norman castle. There is some incredible ornate stonework at Knowth on the kerbstone around the base of the mound. You cannot enter Knowth tomb as it is not safe. Entrance to the Knowth site is via the Brú na Boinne Visitor Centre. The slightly younger cairn at Dowth is not open to the public because it is still being excavated.

Newgrange

Newgrange is the largest site and it dates from 3200 BC. The site is about 500 years older than the Pyramids and about 1500 years older than Stonehenge. It provides an insight into how advanced the Stone Age society was at the time. It contains the largest concentration of Celtic art in Western Europe. According to legend it is the burial place of the High Kings of Tara and the entrance point to the otherworld of the

Tuatha dé Danann. The great grass-covered tomb is about 10m (33ft) high and 85m (280ft) in diameter. The threshold stone with its intricate triple spiral design stands at the entrance. The Newgrange tomb shows how forward-thinking the civilisation was by revealing their interest in cosmology. At dawn on 21 December (the winter solstice and shortest day in the year), the sun shines through a tiny slit in the roof called the 'roof-box' and completely illuminates the inner chamber for 17 minutes (from about 8.58–9.15am). For a few days on either side of the winter solstice, sunlight comes into the chamber. Archaeologists believe that 5,000 years ago the sun would have illuminated a triple spiral design on the end wall of the chamber. There is a ten-year waiting list to see this mystical phenomenon; about 20 people at a time can actually witness the event. For the rest of the year the chamber is completely dark. There are grooves in the stone which slope slightly downwards, allowing water to drain off, keeping the inner chamber dry. The inner chamber has a cruciform shape with a series of tomb niches off it, each with a stone basin to hold the remains. Few bodies were found in the inner chamber and it has been postulated that, perhaps after the illumination during the winter solstice, the bodies were removed because their souls had been released. It is thought that the ancient people of this time worshipped the sun.

WICKLOW MOUNTAINS

Wicklow is known as the garden of Ireland and her green rolling hills are an image that is stereotypical of the Emerald Isle. However, the most beautiful part of the county is the high mountain terrain, which is more like a wasteland than a garden. The mountains are not actually very high, but it is wild country and in the past was impenetrable. Many of the Irish rebels that used to attack Dublin during British rule hid out in the Wicklow Mountains, which have traditionally been known as bandit country. For a visitor to the area, the attractions are the incredible scenery and some great hill walking.

The bog

In spite of the neglect of the boglands and the rather ambivalent attitude of the Irish towards their natural heritage, the bogs of Ireland remain some of the most unusual and rare landscapes on the planet. They were formed during the end of the Ice Age over many centuries from shallow lakes. They are a national treasure, even though they are frequently used as a dumping ground. There are two main types of bog in Ireland: the Atlantic Blanket Bog on the western seaboard and the Mountain Blanket Bog, which is much more widespread. In Wicklow National Park the bog is Mountain Blanket Bog and the best place to see it is from the Military Road around the Sally Gap area of the park and the Liffey Head Bog. The bog here is at the sources of the Liffey, Dargle and Avonmore rivers. The Liffey takes a slow circuitous route through Kildare until it reaches the sea near the Docklands area in Dublin. There is a track through the bog so you can visit the small black pool that is its source.

The Military Road

The Military Road that passes through the Sally Gap has been called the wilderness highway of Ireland. It is the highest public road in the country and was built by the English based at Dublin Castle to try to stem the fast escapes by the rebels Michael Dwyer and Robert Emmet to their mountain hideaways. It was started in 1800 and took nine years to build, but by the time it was finished and the redcoats were marching up and down the road, the rebels had gone. Now it is one of the most scenic roads in the country. It goes from the suburbs of Dublin down to the valley of Glendalough through high and remote mountain country. At the crossroads at Sally Gap if you turn left you will go towards Luggala, which, like Glendalough, is another valley of two lakes. Directly below the road is Loch Tay – part of the Guinness Estate. It is currently owned by Garech a'Bruin who founded Claddagh Records. Some of the more scenic stretches of the Wicklow Way are near the Sally Gap, so you can park the car and head off down a pathway and disappear into the bog for a few hours if you so wish.

The Sugar Loaf Mountains

The two Sugar Loaf Mountains of north Wicklow dominate the skyline as you head south on the DART. You can climb both of these mountains quite easily and the views from the top are very rewarding as you can see for miles on a clear day. There is no public transport so you will need your own transport to get there. Although both of the Sugar Loaf Mountains, especially the larger one, look like ancient volcanoes, they are not volcanic at all.

The Wicklow Way

The Wicklow Way is one of the classic long-distance walking routes in Ireland. It starts in Marlay Park in the suburbs of Dublin and runs north–south through Wicklow County to finally finish in Clonegal, County Carlow. It is 132km (82 miles) long and much of it is believed to run along old pilgrimage routes to Glendalough. It can be walked comfortably in five or six days or, as the locals do, you can do part of the walk in a day.

Getting away from it all

Wicklow's valleys are superlatively green

Shopping

One of the undoubted pleasures of visiting Dublin is the great shopping on offer. As well as clothes, there are many other locally produced goods of quality that will make great presents for your family and friends. If you are a resident of the EU, you must pay VAT on your purchases in Ireland. However, if you are a resident of a non-EU country, you can reclaim VAT on certain purchases.

Shopping hours

The normal shopping hours in Dublin are Monday–Saturday, 9am–6pm. There is late opening on Thursdays until 8pm. In the city centre many shops open on Sundays from noon–6pm, and large shopping centres open late during the week.

What to buy

There is a whole host of great souvenirs to buy in Dublin's shops. From clothing to jewellery and musical instruments to linen, crystal or ceramics, you are guaranteed to be able to buy quality goods and get value for your money.

Traditional Irish clothing products are made of tweed or wool. Tweed jackets, skirts or hats are usually from Donegal. Woollen items include the classic Aran design sweaters. Contemporary designers include John Rocha, Louise Kennedy, Paul Costelloe and Quin & Donnelly. Celtic jewellery is made in both classic and modern designs and comes at prices to suit all

wallets. Irish linen has a worldwide reputation for its excellence and can be simple and elegant in design or elaborately embroidered.

Ceramics are also available in traditional and modern designs. You can buy one-off pieces from small potteries as well as the classic Belleek pottery and Royal Tara china. Irish lead crystal in all its forms is also world famous, with some of the more famous producers including Waterford Crystal and Jerpoint Glass. In addition to the traditional cut-glass designs, John Rocha and Louise Kennedy have worked in a novel collaboration on some modern glass designs.

Buying a bottle of whiskey or Baileys Irish Cream and some farmhouse cheese will also put you in the good books when you get back home.

Some stores will give you a cashback voucher and you can apply to reclaim the VAT at the airport or at the ferry port of your departure as you leave the EU from Ireland.

George's St Arcade

Shopping centres

ILAC Centre

One of the oldest shopping centres in the city centre. Affordable.

Henry St. Tel: (01) 704 1460. www.ilac.ie

Jervis Shopping Centre

Very modern. Dozens of retail outlets.

Mary St. Tel: (01) 878 1323.
www.jervis.ie

Powerscourt Town House

This is as elegant as you can get for a shopping centre in a restored Georgian town house. There is a free tour of the listed building every Fri & Sat at 3pm so you absorb a little history as you browse.

59 South William St. Tel: (01) 671 7000.
www.powerscourtcentre.com

St Stephen's Green Shopping Centre

Elegant wrought-iron architecture skeleton with glass work. It lets in a lot of daylight and gives good views of Grafton St and the people below. Plenty of retail outlets. Located at the heart of the city.

St Stephen's Green West. Tel: (01) 478 0888. www.stephensgreen.com

Traditional retail establishments are to be found alongside the new

Department stores
Arnotts
A recent redesign has revived this store and it is now one of the best-value shops in the city.
12 Henry St. Tel: (01) 805 0400.
www.arnotts.ie
Brown Thomas
Most exclusive store in Dublin. All of the important fashion labels in stock.
88–95 Grafton St. Tel: (01) 605 6666.
www.brownthomas.com
Clerys
Premium and classic designs.
18–27 Lower O'Connell St.
Tel: (01) 878 6000. www.clerys.com
Penneys
One of the cheapest stores in Dublin.

47 Mary St. Tel: (01) 888 0500.
O'Connell St. Tel: (01) 872 0466.

Souvenir shopping
Avoca Handweavers
Upmarket fashions, toys and gifts.
11–13 Suffolk St. Tel: (01) 677 4215.
www.avoca.ie
Blarney Woollen Mills
Handknits, Aran jumpers and linen clothing. Also local crystal and china.
26–27 Nassau St. Tel: (01) 671 0068.
www.blarney.com
Celtic Whiskey Shop
Stocking the best of Ireland's whiskeys – not just Jamesons.
27 Dawson St. Tel: (01) 675 9744.
www.celticwhiskeyshop.com
Cleo
Beautiful woollen and linen clothes for women.
18 Kildare St. Tel: (01) 676 1421.
Crests and Arms
Heraldry and other interesting historical memorabilia including personalised coats of arms.
Parliament Building, 5 Cork Hill,
Dame St. Tel: (01) 616 9000.
House of Ireland
Woollens, Celtic jewellery and Waterford Crystal.
37 Nassau St. Tel: (01) 671 1111.
www.houseofireland.com
Kevin and Howlin Irish Tweeds
Upmarket Donegal tweed specialist.
31 Nassau St. Tel: (01) 677 0257.
www.kevinandhowlin.com
Kilkenny Design Centre
Great for local fashion, jewellery or art.

5–6 Nassau St. Tel: (01) 677 7066.
www.kilkennyshop.com

Markets
George's St Arcade
Covered market. Second-hand clothes and antique jewellery.
Between South Great George's St and Drury St. Open: Mon–Sat 10am–6pm.
Moore St Market
Open air. Fresh fruit, vegetables and cut flowers. Great place for spotting the locals and listening to the chat.
Off Henry St. Open: Mon–Sat.
Smithfield Market
Vegetable and fish market.
Open: Mon–Fri (early).
Temple Bar Food Market
Open air. Organic and alternative goods.
Meeting House Square. Open: Sat 10am–5pm.

Penneys (Mary St) is one of Dublin's cheapest stores

Children

Dublin is definitely a child-friendly city and you may be surprised that children are sometimes let into places that may be considered bastions of adulthood elsewhere. For example, many pubs allow children into them until 6pm and are ideal places to take a break at lunchtime.

The Ark

This is a cultural arts centre specifically for children aged 4–14. There is a special children's theatre and visual art exhibitions.

11A Eustace St, Temple Bar.
Tel: (01) 670 7788. www.ark.ie.
Open: varies according to what's on.
Free admission.
A short walk from the city centre.

Dublin Zoo

The zoo is the most popular of Dublin's tourist attractions. Children love animals and they will get a great thrill out of a visit to the zoo. It was designed by Decimus Burton in 1830 and had only one exhibit when it opened – a wild boar. Now there are many different species of animal, some of which are endangered and undergoing breeding programmes, and after years of it being a very contained space that was rather cruel to the wildlife, it is now a much more open-plan zoo. A recent extension has produced the African Plains section

and it is planned to attain the status of a wildlife park more than a zoo. For children there is a 'Meet the Keeper' programme where you can watch the animals being fed. A famous resident of the Dublin Zoo was the MGM lion that roared to introduce many of their productions. (*See p52.*)

Dublinia and the Viking World

An imaginative and interactive glimpse at the medieval and Viking world. (*See pp48–9.*)

Lambert's Puppet Theatre

There is no better entertainment for young children than a trip to a puppet theatre. If you spent your childhood in Ireland and are returning on holiday, you will definitely have heard of *Wanderly Wagon*, which was a very popular children's television programme on RTE in the 1960s and 1970s. Eugene Lambert, one of the characters in *Wanderly Wagon*, set up a custom-built puppet theatre in his own home. He established the Lambert Puppet Theatre in 1972, which has developed an international reputation for its excellent puppetry. The theatre changes its repertoire on a monthly basis. As well as the traditional tales such as *Little Red Riding Hood*, *Pinocchio* and *Aladdin*, it also puts on some local favourites such as *The Selfish Giant*, written by Oscar Wilde. After a performance, check out the puppet museum upstairs.

Lambert Puppet Theatre, Clifton Lane, Monkstown, Co. Dublin.
Tel: (01) 280 0974. Email:
info@lambertpuppettheatre.ie.
www.lambertpuppettheatre.ie. Check the website for performance times.

Children

Meet the sea lions at Dublin Zoo

The funfair at Merrion Square is a highlight of the St Patrick's Day festival in March

Free admission to the museum after each performance. Bus: 7, 7A, 8. DART: a short walk from Salthill and Monkstown stations.

Seasafari

Tours of Dublin Bay are provided in all-weather ribs (robust motorised dinghies). Wet gear and lifejackets are provided. It is not recommended for children under eight years of age. The

Seasafari expeditions leave from Poolbeg Marina.
114 Ringsend Park. Tel: (01) 668 9802. Email: info@seasafari.ie. www.seasafari.ie. Call first, as operating hours depend largely on the weather.

St Patrick's Day festival

This is without doubt the premier event for children in Dublin. Every year hundreds of thousands of people line the streets to see the parade pass by. There are many other events designed to entertain during the St Patrick's Day festival, including a city-wide treasure hunt and a huge funfair held in Merrion Square.

Viking Splash Tours

This is a novel way to do some sightseeing and is great for children. The tour is in a converted and reconditioned amphibious vehicle called a 'duck', which travels on- and off-road. It starts with a history of ancient Dublin and continues by plunging into the Grand Canal basin for the final part of the tour. Great fun for children over two years of age and adults. The tours leave from Bull Alley St. *Viking Splash Tours, 64–65 St Patrick's St. Tel: (01) 707 6000. Email: info@vikingsplash.ie. www.vikingsplash.com. Season from mid-Feb–end Nov 10am–5pm. Tours leave about every 30 minutes.*

Christmas Events

The **Gaiety** and the **Gate Theatres** hold Christmas pantomimes every year.

Funderland

Each year there is a big funfair held at the Simmonscourt Pavilion of the Royal Dublin Society (RDS) in Ballsbridge from 26 December until the end of January.
Funderland, 97 Henry St.
Tel: (061) 419 988.
Email: info@funfair.ie. www.funfair.ie

Dublin on Ice

Every year a temporary ice rink is set up in Smithfield Plaza over the Christmas period. There is also a festive Christmas market. The ice rink is open from mid-November until early January.
Smithfield on Ice, Smithfield Square.
Tel: (01) 878 8008.
www.dublinonice.ie

Children

St Patrick's Day festival is Dublin's premier event for children

Sport and leisure

The Irish are passionate about sport and their fans are among the best behaved in the world. Some of the best spectator sports in Dublin include soccer internationals, rugby, Gaelic football, hurling and horseracing. There are also plenty of opportunities to participate in sports in Dublin. From golf and sailing to watersports and tennis, there are facilities to suit all tastes. If you are really fit, you might like to try to run the Dublin Marathon in October.

SPECTATOR SPORTS
GAA Museum

In the ultramodern Croke Park stadium, acclaimed from all corners of the architectural world, there is an interactive museum. It provides a comprehensive introduction to the two national sports of Gaelic football and hurling. You can even have a go at the sports themselves. A word of warning – hurling is not as easy as it looks.
Clonliffe Rd, Croke Park.
Tel: (01) 819 2323.
www.gaa.ie/museum. Open: daily
9.30am–5pm. Admission charge.
Guided tours take place daily.
Call for times. Bus: 3, 11, 16 from
O'Connell St.

Gaelic football and hurling

Gaelic football (often abbreviated by the locals to GAA) is one of the two Irish national sports. It is most similar to Australian Rules Football, and Ireland and Australia do play each other at a hybrid game called

International Rules. Dublin is one of the top teams in the country.

Hurling is the other national sport and is the fastest field game. It is played with a wooden stick called a *hurley* and a very hard small ball called a *sliotar*. The Dublin hurling team is traditionally less successful. The finals of the Gaelic football and hurling championships are played at Croke Park Stadium in September, but the event is so popular that you are unlikely to be able to purchase a ticket. The games are broadcast live on national TV and radio.
For further information contact the
Gaelic Athletic Association. Tel: (01) 836
3222. www.gaa.ie

Greyhound racing

For an alternative sporting experience, you could go greyhound racing. This sport is popular in Ireland and the UK. There are two venues in Dublin:
Harold's Cross Stadium (*151 Harold's Cross Rd. Tel: (01) 497 1081*) and

153

Sport and leisure

Shelbourne Park Greyhound Stadium
(*Shelbourne Park. Tel: 1 890 829 839*).
The season is from February to early
December, and race meetings are held
two to three times a week.

The Horse Show

The Royal Dublin Society (RDS) hold
their annual horse show in August at
the RDS Showgrounds in Ballsbridge.
The showjumping, dressage and the
fashion on Ladies' Day are the
highlights of the show.
*Royal Dublin Society Showgrounds,
Ballsbridge. Tel: (01) 668 0866.
www.dublinhorseshow.com*

Horseracing

The Irish love their horses and they
love to gamble. It thus comes as no
surprise that horseracing is one of the
most popular spectator sports in the
country. There are many racecourses
only a short distance from Dublin,
including: **Leopardstown** (*Tel: (01) 289
0500. www.leopardstown.com*),
Fairyhouse (*Tel: (01) 825 6167.
www.fairyhouseracecourse.ie*),
The Curragh (*Tel: (045) 441 205.
www.curragh.ie*) and **Laytown** (*Tel:
(041) 984 2111*). The major race
meetings are the **Easter Meeting** at
Fairyhouse (with the Irish Grand
National on Easter Monday), the
Steeplechase Festival in April at the
Curragh and the **Christmas Meeting** at
Leopardstown from 26 to 29 December.
In the summertime there are races on
the beach at Laytown, which is one of
the world's few officially recognised
racing tracks on a beach.
*For further information, contact
Horseracing Ireland, The Curragh,
Co. Kildare. Tel: (045) 842 800.
Email: info@hri.ie. www.goracing.ie*

Rugby

Although not as popular as soccer,
rugby is still a favourite spectator sport
in Dublin. One of the best times to
come to Dublin is for a rugby weekend
when the national team is playing at
home in the Six Nations Tournament.
There is friendly rivalry between the
fans, and the atmosphere in the streets
and pubs before and after the matches
can be electric. It is obviously better
when Ireland win, which nowadays is
a little more often than before. The
undoubted highlight is when the

The high-speed national game of hurling

English team comes to play in the city, as the rivalry is most intense between Ireland and England. International rugby games have traditionally been played at **Lansdowne Road**. This venerable stadium is currently being redeveloped into a new 50,000-capacity all-seater stadium, and internationals will be played at Croke Park until renovations are completed in early 2010. However, tickets are like gold dust. The Province of Leinster (the Lions) play rugby at the **RDS** in the European League (Heineken Cup) and Celtic League. They are one of the top club teams in Europe. Again, because of the popularity of the game, it is difficult to get tickets.

Football

Dubliners are fanatical about football and support their national team above all else. If the national team is playing in Dublin, they usually play at Lansdowne Road. During the renovations, though, internationals will also be played at Croke Park. Many Irish soccer fans support teams in the English Premier League and most top Irish players play for the top teams in the Premier League. Current leading Dublin players include Damien Duff,

Boating is popular in Dublin Bay

who plays for Fulham, and Robbie Keane, who plays for Tottenham Hotspur. Standards of the local Football Association of Ireland (FAI) soccer league are improving all the time. *For information about international fixtures or games in the local league contact the FAI. Tel: (01) 703 7500. www.fai.ie*

SPORTING ACTIVITIES
The Dublin Marathon

The Dublin City Marathon is held at the end of October. It attracts an international field, both amateur and professional, as thousands of runners take over the streets of Dublin in a display of unprecedented fitness. *For further information contact the Dublin City Marathon Office. Tel: (01) 623 2250. www.dublinmarathon.ie*

Golf

Golf is one of the biggest participation sports in Ireland. High-profile Dubliner golfers on the international scene include Padraig Harrington and Paul McGinley, who inspire a whole nation of hackers. There are many good golf courses within a short distance of Dublin city. Some are among the best golf courses in the world, so the green fee can be expensive. In September 2006 Ireland played host to the Ryder Cup at the K Club in Kildare. *For further information contact the Golfing Union of Ireland. National Headquarters, Carton Demesne,*

Maynooth, County Kildare. Tel: (01) 601 6842. Email: information@gui.ie. www.gui.ie

Druids Glen Golf Club
Newtownmountkennedy, Co. Wicklow. Tel: (01) 2873600. Email: info@druidsglen.ie. www.druidsglen.ie

The European Club
Brittas Bay, Co. Wicklow. Tel: (0404) 47415. Email: www.golfeurope.com/clubs/european

The K Club
Straffan, Co. Kildare. Tel: (01) 601 7200. www.kclub.com

Portmarnock Hotel and Golf Links
Portmarnock. Tel: (01) 846 2968. www.portmarnockgolfclub.ie

Sailing and watersports

Dublin Bay is a great place to go sailing, canoeing and windsurfing. For information on how to go sailing in the bay contact the **Irish Sailing Association** (*Tel: (01) 280 0239. Email: info@sailing.ie. www.sailing.ie*). The **Irish Disabled Sailing Association** will provide you with information if you have a disability (*Tel: 087 254 6880. Email: sail@sailforce.ie. www.sailforce.ie*). For information on windsurfing contact the **Irish Windsurfing Association** (*www.windsurfing.ie*).

Sport and leisure

Food and drink

The upside of the notoriously damp climate of Ireland is that the country produces some of the finest-quality foodstuffs in the entire world. The rich pasturelands provide ideal grazing for cattle and sheep, and the extensive coastline and unpolluted rivers provide myriad varieties of fish. Because of the quality of meat, particularly beef, and for various other cultural reasons, traditional cooking has been the mainstay of Irish cuisine until very recently.

WHAT TO EAT
Glossary of food and drink
Bacon and cabbage

The stereotypical Irish dish consists of boiled bacon and cabbage, usually served with boiled potatoes. Although it is still eaten on St Patrick's Day throughout the world, it is not as popular as it used to be in Ireland.

Baileys Irish Cream

The world-famous blend of Irish whiskey and cream. It is usually taken with ice.

Barm brack

A tea cake (more like bread) eaten at Halloween. It contains a lucky ring that will guarantee you get married soon. The secret to good brack is soaking the fruit in a pot of Irish tea overnight.

Beef and Guinness® pie

This recipe is beef cooked in a pie with a special Guinness® gravy. Not everybody approves of it and some

traditionalists feel it is sacrilege to use Guinness® in this way.

Boxty

An Irish potato pancake served with a savoury filling of either meat or vegetables.

Brown bread

There are many brown bread recipes in Ireland and they vary considerably in quality.

Cheese

A decade ago Ireland only produced a handful of great cheeses, with most people eating processed and Cheddar cheeses. But that has all changed and there are now countless excellent Irish cheeses on the market. Some of these are Irish versions of traditional French and Dutch cheeses. Nowadays Irish cheese is not just made from cow's milk – some tasty varieties are organically produced from sheep's and goat's milk. The range of tastes is infinite and some of the cheeses you might try include Cashel Blue, Durrus, Carrigaline, St Killian, Gubbeen (the smoked variety is recommended), Dubliner, Coolie, Cooleeney Camembert and Adrahan.

Christmas cake

Every Irish family seems to have its own recipe for this traditional fruit cake eaten only at Christmas. The cake is covered in a layer of almond icing and white icing.

Christmas dinner

The traditional Christmas dinner in Ireland is turkey, ham and spiced beef with croquette potatoes, Brussels sprouts and other vegetables.

Christmas pudding

This is an extremely rich, steamed fruit pudding that is eaten with cream or brandy butter. After two helpings it is usually not possible to move until New Year's Day.

Cockles and mussels

Local shellfish that feature in the song about Molly Malone. They are usually cooked in white wine or garlic butter.

Coddle

Chopped sausages and rashers of fried bacon cooked in a stock with vegetables.

Coffee

Although you may be unlucky and get cheap instant coffee in some places, this is no longer the norm. Dubliners have embraced coffee drinking and become more European in their tastes. There is tremendous variety on offer in the many new cafés that have sprung up.

Ireland also produces fine wines

Colcannon

This delicious dish is traditionally
served at Halloween, which was the
start of the Celtic year in ancient times.
It consists of curly kale, potatoes, milk
and butter. Sometimes coins or a ring
are put into the dish for good luck, so
be careful you don't swallow them.

Corned beef and cabbage

Corned beef (salted beef brisket) is
eaten with cabbage. As with boiled
bacon, it is eaten on St Patrick's Day
more by foreigners than by the
Irish themselves. The beef was
traditionally salted before the time
of refrigeration.

Cruibin

These are pickled pigs' trotters, usually
boiled with carrots and herbs. They are
an acquired taste and not many
restaurants will serve them now.

Dublin Bay prawns

Sweet local prawns served in a prawn
cocktail or a variety of dishes, but can
taste best when simply cooked in
garlic butter.

Fish and chips

Deep-fried fish and chipped potatoes
can be eaten as a takeaway or in
restaurants. Salt and vinegar are the
common condiments used to flavour
the meal, but some restaurants also
have tartare. Cod is the most common
fish, but whiting and plaice (a local flat
fish) are also used. The cod stocks in

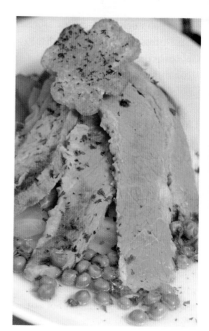

Corned beef and cabbage will make a hearty
meal

the Irish seas are dwindling so the cod
option may not be on the menu for
long. Deep-fried scampi (a small prawn
in batter) is also commonly seen. The
quality of the food presented depends
on the location and the freshness of the
fish. If you are eating in the fishing port
of Howth, this could be the best dish
you choose and the best food you have
when in Dublin.

Full Irish breakfast

There are so many variations on a full
Irish, but the basic ingredients are a fry
of rashers, sausages, a fried egg, grilled
tomato, black and white pudding and
perhaps a potato cake.

Guinness® stout

The quintessential Dublin tipple has to be tried at least once. It is best to order a half-pint glass rather than a pint if you have never tasted it before. There are two other common Irish stouts produced in Cork in the south of Ireland: Murphy's and Beamish. You can get them in some Dublin pubs, but not all pubs serve these stouts as some are partisan to the locally produced Guinness®.

Hot whiskey/port

Traditional winter warmers served in most pubs during the winter, especially at Christmas time. Although there are slight variations, both are usually served with hot water, sugar and lemon. They are also taken for medicinal purposes.

Irish coffee

This is an extremely moreish drink made from whiskey, coffee and cream. It is a traditional Christmas drink. Just like pouring Guinness®, the making of an Irish coffee is an art form, and if made properly it will taste smooth and heavenly.

Irish stew

Originally a poor man's dish made from mutton or lamb and onions, with a potato topping.

Oysters and Guinness®

There is no middle ground with oysters. Jonathan Swift's view was, 'He was a bold man that ever first ate oysters.' You either love them or hate them and they can be an acquired taste. One of the best

Enjoy traditional Irish stew with a pint of Guinness®

ways to have oysters, and the local way, is with a pint of Guinness®.

Porridge

A traditional breakfast cereal made from oats that, if prepared properly, is smooth and creamy. If you cannot handle the cholesterol load of a full Irish or are vegetarian, you might want to consider porridge as an alternative. It can be served in a number of ways including with added salt and milk or the much sweeter option with cream and a little sugar or honey.

Porter cake

A dark fruit cake made with Guinness®.

Scones

Irish scones can be white or brown and are usually served with butter and home-made jam. They also sometimes come with cream and usually contain sultanas.

Smoked salmon

Irish salmon is right up there with the best. Good wild Irish smoked salmon will almost melt in the mouth. Frequently served with a fresh salad and brown bread.

Soda bread

A traditional bread (brown or white) where baking soda is used instead of yeast. Buttermilk should be used.

Spiced beef

Part of the Christmas dinner, a mixture of spices is used and, of course, a drop of Guinness®.

Tea

The Irish love their tea and they drink more cups per capita than any other nation in the world. You might feel some Irish were born with a cup of tea attached to their hand. A cup of tea will cure all ills and provides just enough time for a chat. Tea is taken well brewed with milk.

Tripe and onions

This one is for those with a strong constitution. Tripe is the lining of a cow's stomach and is cooked slowly with milk and onions.

Whiskey

Irish whiskey is world famous. As well as the most popular brands (Jameson's, Black Bush, Bushmills, Powers and Paddy), you might try some of the lesser-known but delicious brands (Midleton, Tirconnell, Kilbeggan and Redbreast).

A chaser is when you have a measure of whiskey along with your pint of Guinness® just to keep it company.

WHERE TO EAT

Not so long ago Dublin was a cultural backwater as far as cuisine was concerned, and there was very little choice for dining out. This is no longer the case; just as the cultural mix of the city has altered, so have the dining habits of the city's inhabitants. For the visitor

Irish whiskey is so distinctive because it is triple distilled

to the city there is plenty of choice and practically every cuisine is represented. Even traditional Irish food has undergone a revolution, with a whole range of eclectic new recipes invented by the city's most creative chefs.

Dining in Dublin magazine, distributed free of charge in Dublin hotels, is a useful restaurant guide and will give you some of the menus on offer at the top restaurants. If you so desire, you can decide exactly what you want to eat before you leave your room.

Prices for a meal

Irish restaurants have something of a reputation for being overpriced and poor value for money. Since March 2003, the Restaurants Association of Ireland has encouraged restaurants to have a Special Value Menu, which is a fixed-price set menu for either lunch or dinner. Restaurants that agree to introduce the menu are listed in a special guide distributed at Tourist Information Centres throughout the country. Some top restaurants offer a two-course set menu for €20 and a three-course set menu for €30. The star categories below give a rough idea of the cost of a meal for two, with wine included. Prices are subject to inflation and this should only be used as a guide.

★	Under €60
★★	€60–80
★★★	€80–100
★★★★	over €100

BEST FOR TRADITIONAL BREAKFAST

Bean Scene ★

This Ballsbridge café has some excellent traditional fare for a very reasonable price. Cheap and cheerful.
4 Haddington Rd.
Tel: (01) 667 5522.
Open: Mon–Fri 7am–3.30pm, Sat–Sun 9am–4pm.

Bewley's Oriental Café ★

Breakfast at Bewley's has been a Dublin institution since its opening in 1967. Although it has lost a little of its authenticity with the influx of tourists, the breakfast is still among the best in the city.
78–79 Grafton St.
Tel: (01) 672 7720.
Open: Mon–Thur 8am–10pm, Fri–Sat 8am–11pm, Sun 9am–10pm. Breakfast served until noon.

The Bridge Café ★

Full Irish available most of the day.
47 Shelbourne Rd, Ballsbridge.
Tel: (01) 660 8632.
Open: Mon–Sat 9am–5pm, Sun 10am–5pm.

COFFEE, A SNACK AND A CHAT

Dublin has embraced the European café culture. There are quite simply hundreds of excellent small cafés, from traditional to trendy, and the quality of the food is high. Here are just a few of the recommended establishments.

Cobalt Café & Gallery ★
16 North Great George's St. Tel: (01) 873 0313.
Open: Mon–Fri 8am–4pm.

Irish Film Institute ★
6 Eustace St.
Tel: (01) 679 3477.
www.irishfilm.ie.
Open: daily 10am–6pm.

Joy of Coffee ★
25 Essex St (in Temple Bar). Tel: (01) 679 3393.
Open: daily 9am–10pm (later at weekends).

Lemon ★
Great sweet and savoury crêpes, and they are authentic too.
66 South William St.
Tel: (01) 672 9044.
Open: Mon–Fri 8am–9.30pm, Sat 8am–7.30pm, Sun 10am–6pm.

National Gallery Café ★
Millennium Wing. Tel: (01) 661 5133. Open: daily.

Queen of Tarts ★

A Victorian delight with some nice pastries.
4 Cork Hill.
Tel: (01) 670 7499. Open: Mon–Fri 7.30am–7pm, Sat–Sun 9am–7pm.

The Terrace Café ★
National Concert Hall, Earlsfort Terrace.
Tel: (01) 478 5005.
Email: nch@kylemore.ie.
Open: daily 9am–5.30pm.

RESTAURANTS AND FINE DINING

Fast food

There is a preponderance of fast-food restaurants in Dublin, particularly on O'Connell St. If you like this kind of cuisine you will be able to get what you want as most major fast-food chains are represented. The recommendation here is for the best takeaway fish and chip place in Dublin city centre, as the other takeaways produce universal fare.

Leo Burdocks ★

This place is fast food at its best and a Dublin institution. In times gone by the temperamental owner would only open up when there was a huge

queue outside, but that is no longer the case. It is arguably the best takeaway fish and chip establishment in Ireland. The queues can be long as it is a bit of a tourist trap.
2 Werburgh St.
Tel: (01) 454 0306.
www.leoburdocks.com.
Open: Mon–Fri 12.30–11pm, Sat 2–11pm.

Traditional Irish food
Gallagher's Boxty House ★
Traditional potato pancakes (boxty) are the speciality, but there are other traditional dishes on the menu.
20–21 Temple Bar.
Tel: (01) 677 2762.
www.boxtyhouse.ie.
Open: 9am–11pm.
Gruel ★
Despite the name, the food is good and very cheap. One of the best-value places in town. Menu from stews to salads to pizza.
69 Dame St.
Tel: (01) 670 7119.
Open: daily 7am–10pm.
Millstone Restaurant ★★
An unusual but effective combination of pizzeria and traditional Irish

cuisine in atmospheric surroundings.
39 Dame St.
Tel: (01) 679 9931.
Open: daily 10.30am–midnight.
O'Connells ★★★★
Traditional Irish food and seafood. Early bird menu.
Ballsbridge Court Hotel, Lansdown Rd, Ballsbridge.
Tel: (01) 665 5940.
www.oconnellsballsbridge.com. Open: Mon–Sat 7.30am–10pm, Sun 8am–9pm.

Modern Irish
The Church ★★
A very recent conversion from church into bar, café and restaurant serving modern Irish and coeliac-friendly food.
St Mary's Church, Mary St.
Tel: (01) 828 0102.
Open (food service): Main Bar Mon–Wed noon–9.30pm, Thur–Sat noon–10pm, Sun 12.30–8pm; Cellar Bar & Tower Bar Mon–Sat noon–10pm, Sun 12.30–10pm; Gallery Restaurant Mon–Wed noon–10pm, Thur–Sat noon–11pm, Sun 12.30–10pm.

The Market Bar ★★
An interesting addition to the Irish Mediterranean fusion cuisine scene, with largely Spanish influence.
14A Fade St.
Tel: (01) 613 9094.
www.marketbar.ie.
Open (food service): Mon–Thur noon–11.30pm, Fri–Sat noon–12.30am, Sun 3–11pm.
Seagrass ★★
Young restaurant with a growing reputation. Modern Irish food with some excellent early evening offers.
30 South Richmond St.
Tel: (01) 478 9595.
www.seagrassdublin.com.
Closed: Mon.
Roly's Bistro ★★★
A Dublin institution offering the very best in traditional fare with a contemporary twist.
7 Ballsbridge Terrace.
Tel: (01) 668 2611.
www.rolysbistro.ie.
Open: daily noon–2.45pm & 6–9.45pm.
The Schoolhouse ★★★
Modern Irish and international cuisine.
2–8 Northumberland Rd.

Tel: (01) 667 5014.
www.schoolhouse.ie.
Open: 12.30–3pm &
6–10pm. Closed: lunch
Sat & Sun.

American
Shanahan's on the Green ★★★★

Sumptuous Georgian-style dining in a classic and exclusive American steakhouse. The best steak in town.
119 St Stephen's Green.
Tel: (01) 407 0939.
www.shanahans.ie.
Open for dinner from 6pm.

Continental
Bad Ass Café ★

Great value for pizza and pasta dishes. Sinéad O'Connor once worked here as a waitress.
9–11 Crown Alley.
Tel: (01) 671 2596.
Open: 8am–11pm.

The Italian Corner ★★

Excellent European-style menu. Great view of the Liffey. Live music Wednesday to Sunday.
23–24 Wellington Quay.
Tel: (01) 671 9114.
www.theitaliancorner.ie.
Open: daily 8am–11pm.

Soup Dragon ★★

Not a restaurant at all really, but the range of delicious soups on offer makes this place worth a mention – a great place for lunch.
168 Capel St.
Tel: (01) 872 3277.
Open: Mon–Fri 8am–
4.30pm, Sat 11am–4pm.

Salamanca ★★/★★★

Dublin's long-established tapas restaurant, serving authentic Spanish cuisine. Eat early from one of the daily specials or the little tower of tapas, or come late and enjoy the flamenco music. Either way, be prepared to queue or make a reservation beforehand. Music and dancing daily in summer, weekends and Mondays in winter.
1 St Andrew's St.
Tel: (01) 677 4799.
www.salamanca.ie.
Open: Mon–Sat noon–
late, Sun 1pm–late.

The Saddle Room ★★★

Lovely place for a romantic dinner for two or an evening out with friends and family. This place has the confidence and space to cater for anyone's needs. Far more than just a steak and seafood restaurant. Food is thoughtfully cooked, unfussy and comes in decent portions. Nothing haute here. Two courses for lunch is easily affordable and adequate.
Shelbourne Hotel,
27 St Stephen's Green.
Tel: (01) 663 4500.

Chapter One ★★★★

Upmarket dining. Excellent service in this top-of-the-range restaurant.
18–19 Parnell Square
(in the basement of the
Dublin Writer's Museum).
Tel: (01) 873 2266. www.
chapteronerestaurant.com.
Open: Tue–Fri 12.30–2pm
& 6–11pm, Sat 6–11pm.

French cuisine
Café Leon ★★

The cuisine veers towards modern European, but the atmosphere is genuinely French and if you tune out the Dublin voices you could imagine yourself in Paris. Good offers on two-course meals.
33 Exchequer St.
Tel: 01 670 7238.
www.cafeleon.ie. Open:
Mon–Sat 8am–10pm, Sun
10am–10pm.

L'Ecrivain ★★★★

Top and exclusive

restaurant. French cuisine with an Irish flavour for a really special treat.
109 Lower Baggot St.
Tel: (01) 661 1919.
Open: Mon–Fri 12.30–2.30pm & 7–10pm, Sat 7–10pm.

L'Gueuleton ★★★★
The latest French kid on the block, which has been getting rave reviews.
1 Fade St.
Tel: (01) 675 3708.
Open: Mon–Sat 12.30–2.45pm & 6–10pm.

Restaurant Patrick Guilbaud ★★★★
The ultimate in quality French cuisine. The finest of Dublin restaurants.
21 Upper Merrion St.
Tel: (01) 676 4192.
Open: Tue–Sat 12.30–2.15pm & 7.30–10.15pm.

Italian cuisine
Steps of Rome ★
The place where Italians eat in Dublin, with real pizza.
Unit 1, Chatham St.
Tel: (01) 670 5630.
Open: Mon–Sat noon–11pm, Sun 1–10pm.

Botticelli ★★
Authentic Italian food in a long-established

restaurant. Excellent ice-cream parlour next door run by the same people.
3 Temple Bar.
Tel: (01) 672 7289.
www.botticelli.ie.
Open:12.30pm–midnight.

Asian
Wagamama ★★
An extensive choice of healthy noodle dishes.
South King St.
Tel: (01) 478 2152.
www.wagamama.com.
Open: Mon–Sat noon–11pm, Sun noon–10pm.

Sinners ★★/★★★
One of Dublin's longest established restaurants, this place serving authentic Lebanese food is a little gem. Try the excellent Lebanese version of tapas – *mezze* – or go for one of the mildly spiced main dishes served with vegetables and tabouleh. Excellent early-bird offers. Bellydancing Friday and Saturday evenings.
Parliament St.
Tel (01) 675 0050.
www.sinners.ie.
Open: daily 5pm–late.

Thai Orchid ★★★
Largest Thai restaurant in Ireland. Excellent

authentic Thai food and good service. Reasonable early-bird menu.
7 Westmoreland St.
Tel: (01) 671 9969.
Fax: (01) 671 9968.
Open: lunch, Mon–Fri 12.30–2.30pm; dinner, Sun–Thur 5–11pm, Fri & Sat 5pm–midnight.

Yamamori ★★★
Japanese soups, noodle dishes and sushi.
71–72 South Great George's St.
Tel: (01) 475 5001.
Open: daily noon–11pm.

Vegetarian and wholefood
Blazing Salads ★★
Good salads and vegetarian dishes.
42 Drury St.
Tel: (01) 671 9552.
Open: Mon–Sat 9.30am–6pm.

Juice Café ★★
Funky vegetarian restaurant-cum-café.
73–83 South Great George's St.
Tel: (01) 475 7856.
Open: 11am–11pm.

Cornucopia ★★★
Good and healthy wholefood and vegetarian fare. Check out the breakfasts here.

19 Wicklow St.
Tel: (01) 677 7583.
Open Mon–Sat 8.30am–
8pm, Sun noon–7pm.

RESTAURANTS IN THE GREATER DUBLIN AREA

Cape Greko ★★

Hidden away upstairs above a pizza place, this is a little bit of Cyprus at the Irish seaside. All the Greek classics, lots of vegetarian options, children welcome before 9pm, music on Friday nights. The early-bird menu makes it a good bargain to boot.
Unit 1, First Floor,
New Street, Malahide.
Tel: (01) 845 6288.
www.capegreko.ie

Abbey Tavern ★★★

Great local seafood caught fresh by Howth anglers.
28 Abbey St, Howth.
Tel: (01) 839 0307.
Open: Mon–Sat
6pm–late, bar food
noon–late.

Johnnie Fox's ★★★

A Dublin institution with some excellent seafood and some great traditional entertainment. Get

directions if you are driving, or better still take a taxi.
Glencullen, The Dublin
Mountains, Co. Dublin.
Tel: (01) 295 5647.
www.jfp.ie. Open: Mon–
Sat noon–11.30pm, Sun
noon–11pm.

Nosh ★★★

Superb international cuisine with excellent service.
111 Coliemore Rd,
Dalkey, Co. Dublin.
Tel: (01) 284 0666.
Open: Tue–Sun noon–4pm
& 6–10pm. Closed: Mon.

King Sitric Fish Restaurant ★★★★

Gourmet fish restaurant with freshly caught produce on the menu.
East Pier, Howth.
Tel: (01) 832 5235/6729.
Email: info@kingsitric.ie.
www.kingsitric.ie. Open:
Mon & Wed–Sat
6.30pm–late. Closed: Sun
& Public Holidays.

PUBS, CLUBS AND NIGHTLIFE

The best night out in Dublin is likely to be in one of its famous pubs, but there are plenty of other nocturnal activities on offer, from the

cultural to the downright hedonistic.

To see Dubliners at their best you really must spend one night in a famous drinking establishment. This is where they let their hair down and you are most likely to experience some spontaneous hospitality. There are so many pubs to choose from that you are guaranteed to find your own personal favourite and end up a regular before your holiday is over. Irish pubs no longer have that suffocating smoky atmosphere since the smoking ban was introduced.

Some bars in Dublin may feel as if they are male-only establishments because of the large number of men in the bar, but women are generally welcome in any establishment and should not feel intimidated (ask your hotel for a recommendation). Like anywhere it is always safer with a companion rather than alone and there are some areas of Dublin – particularly around O'Connell St, Mountjoy Square, Gardiner St and near Christ Church – where women should be particularly careful late at night, even in a group. *Normal opening hours: Sun–Wed 11.30am– 11.30pm, Thur–Sat 11.30am–12.30am.*

TRADITIONAL IRISH PUBS
Bars for food
The Brazen Head

Oldest pub in town, or at least on the site of what was allegedly the oldest pub. Good pub lunches. Can get a little touristy in high season, and not as authentic as it could be. *20 Bridge St. Tel: (01) 677 9549. www.brazenhead.com. Open: 11.30am–12.30am.*

Davy Byrnes

Literary pub with 'gourmet' dining connections. Great for Gorgonzola sandwiches as per its 'Bloomsday' connection. *21 Duke St. Tel: (01) 677 5217. www.davybyrnes.com. Open: 11.30am–12.30am.*

O'Neills

Popular and unpretentious drinking hole. Hard to get a seat at night, but this is the same with most popular Dublin pubs. Excellent carvery lunch. *2 Suffolk St. Tel: (01) 679 3656. Open: 11.30am–12.30am.*

Sinnotts

Large underground bar with a great atmosphere. Carvery lunch and evening food. *South King St. Tel: (01) 478 4698. Open: 11.30am–12.30am.*

Bars for long chats and pints
Grogan's

A truly democratic crowd in this old Dublin institution. *15 South William St. Tel: (01) 677 9320. Open: 11.30am–12.30am.*

John Kavanagh's

Better known to its many fans as The Gravediggers, this place has been run by the same family for six generations. No music, no TV, no themes – just a reputation for excellent beer. Customers politely leave their glasses

The light from the interior of an Irish pub beckons you in to experience the *craic*

on the ledge of the cemetery wall after the bar has closed for the night.
1 Prospect Square, Glasnevin. Tel: (01) 830 7978. Open: Sun–Wed 11.30am–11pm, Thur–Sat 11.30am–12.30am.

The Long Hall

Victorian-style pub with good pints and a really long bar.
51 South Great George's St. Tel: (01) 475 1590. Open: 11.30am–12.30am.

Mulligans

The quintessential Dublin pub and a veritable institution. There is a strong argument for this pub's bartenders being the best in Dublin, and so the Guinness® is better than good. There is no music and absolutely no singing permitted.
8 Poolbeg St. Tel: (01) 677 5582. Open: Mon–Wed 10.30am–11.30pm, Thur–Sat 10.30am–12.30am, Sun 12.30–11.30pm.

The Palace Bar

A small and unpretentious typical Dublin pub. Another favourite with former literary greats and currently with students.

Traditional Irish session on Wednesday nights.
21 Fleet St. Tel: (01) 677 9290. Open: Mon–Wed 10.30am–11.30pm, Thur–Sat 10.30am–12.30am, Sun 12.30–11pm.

Porter House

Pub with its own brewery. Great selection of beers. Check out the oyster stout.
Parliament St. Tel: (01) 679 8850. Open: Mon–Wed 10.30am–11.30pm, Thur–Sat 10.30am–12.30am, Sun 12.30–11pm.

Toners

Another great traditional haunt with snugs. W B Yeats paid his one single visit to a Dublin pub here. He had a glass of sherry and left. He was not too impressed with the experience.
139 Lower Baggot St. Tel: (01) 676 3090. Open: Mon–Wed & Sun 11.30am–11.30pm, Thur–Sat 11.30am–12.30am.

Bars for traditional music

Auld Dubliner

Traditional music sessions every day.

24–25 Temple Bar. Tel: (01) 677 0527. Open: Sun–Thur 10.30am–12.30am, Fri–Sat 10.30am–2.30am.

Cobblestone

Set amidst the building works of the Smithfield redevelopment project, Cobblestone is probably the most authentic live traditional music venue in the city. Tiny, unreconstructed bar and performance area upstairs. Check out the website for what's on before you visit.
77 King St North. Tel: (01) 872 1799. www.myspace.com/ thecobblestone

Johnnie Fox's

Traditional Irish music every night of the week. There is also a traditional 'hooley' (musical entertainment) with Irish dancing.
Glencullen, The Dublin Mountains, Co. Dublin. Tel: (01) 295 5647. www.jfp.ie. Open: Mon–Sat 10.30am–11.30pm, Sun noon–11.30pm.

O'Donoghues

The pub that launched The Dubliners is a real music treasure. Catch a

session here before you leave Dublin.
15 Merrion Row.
Tel: (01) 660 7194.
www.odonoghues.ie.
Open: 11.30am–12.30am.

The Oliver St John Gogarty
A bit of a tourist trap but still a good place to hear traditional music over a pint.
58–59 Fleet St, Temple Bar.
Tel: (01) 671 1822.
www.gogartys.ie.
Open: 10.30am–2.30am.

The Temple Bar
Popular drinking hole. Live music every night of the week. Beer garden.
47–48 Temple Bar.
Tel: (01) 672 5287.
Open: 11.30am–12.30am.

Sports bars
All Sports Bar
Friendly place with TV screens and sporting paraphernalia.
Fleet St. Tel: (01) 679 3942.

The Old Stand
A traditional haunt for sports fans, it gets packed whenever any local sporting events are on. Arrive early and soak up the atmosphere, which can get boisterous.

37 Exchequer St.
Tel: (01) 677 7220.
Open: 11am–12.30am.

Bars for rock music
Eamonn Doran's
Used to be the Rock Garden venue which launched more than a few musical careers.
3A Crown Alley.
Tel: (01) 679 9114.
Open: 11am–3pm, nightclub 8pm–3am.

The International Bar
Specialises in acoustic rock music.
23 Wicklow St.
Tel: (01) 677 9250. Open: Sun–Thur 10.30am–11.30pm, Fri–Sat 10.30am–12.30am.

MODERN BARS
The Dragon
A relatively recent new gay bar and club.
South Great George's St.
Tel: (01) 478 1590. Open: Mon, Thur, Fri & Sat 5pm–2.30am, Tue–Wed 5pm–11.30pm, Sun 5–11pm.

Fitzsimons
Floors and floors of places to drink to assorted DJs. Occasional live bands. Roof terrace and nightclub.

15–18 East Essex St, Temple Bar.
Tel: (01) 677 9135.
www.fitzsimonshotel.com

The Morgan
Stylish bar, popular with office crowds on their way home from work. Nice bar food and some quirky decorations.
10 Fleet St, Temple Bar.
Tel: (01) 643 7000.
www.themorgan.com

Ron Black's
The coolest kid on the Dawson Street block. People queue to get in here at weekends and it's just a pub. Classy place, nice music.
37 Dawson St.
Tel: (01) 672 8231.
www.ronblacks.ie

Turks Head Chop House
A trendy café bar with hip DJs. Belly dancing during the summer.
Corner of Parliament St and Essex St.
Tel: (01) 679 9701.
Open: daily noon–3am.

Zanzibar
Lavishly decorated in an Eastern style.
36 Lower Ormond Quay.
Tel: (01) 878 7212.
www.capitalbars.com.
Open: daily 4pm–3am.

Entertainment

There's a wealth of entertainment options in Dublin, from theatre performances to music gigs and blockbuster movies. Tickets for concerts and gigs can be obtained online from Ticketmaster (www.ticketmaster.ie).

Cinemas
Cineworld
Parnell Centre, Parnell St.
Tel: 1 520 880 444. www.cineworld.ie
Irish Film Institute
Arthouse-orientated.
6 Eustace St. Tel: (01) 679 5744.
Savoy
Upper O'Connell St. Tel: (0818) 221 122.
Screen
D'Olier St. Tel: (0818) 221 122.

Comedy clubs
Capital Comedy Club
Resident compere and visiting comics. Sundays and Wednesdays 9pm to 11.15pm. Small venue, so wise to book. *Ha'penny Bridge Inn, Wellington Quay. Tel: (01) 677 0616. www.capitalcomedyclub.com*
The International Comedy Club
Long-standing alternative comedy venue, now six nights a week and twice on Saturdays. Good value for money in a lovely old unreconstructed pub. Times vary, so check for details. *23 Wicklow St. Tel: (01) 677 9250. www.internationalcomedyclub.com*

Concert venues
There are often summer gigs in the Phoenix Park and at Slane Castle.
The Button Factory
Top venue for all kinds of arts. *Curved St, Temple Bar. Tel: (01) 670 9202. Email: info@tbcm.ie. www.tbmc.ie. Open: 9.30am–2.30am.*
Crawdaddy
Part of a complex of clubs and live music venues, Crawdaddy hosts live music. *Old Railway Station, Harcourt St. Tel: (01) 476 3374. www.pod.ie*
The Helix
Shiny, new-ish state-of-the-art concert venue, for everything from reality pop contests to Cliff Richard, theatre performances, visiting orchestras and much more, in three performance spaces. *DCU, Collins Avenue, Glasnevin. Tel: (01) 700 7000. www.thehelix.ie*

National Concert Hall
Classical music.
Earlsfort Terrace. Tel: (01) 417 0077.
www.nch.ie

O₂
Leading venue for big pop and rock acts.
East Link Bridge, North Wall Quay.
Tel: (0818) 719 391. www.theo2.ie

Vicar Street
Award-winning venue for live music
and comedy; visiting big names.
58–59 Thomas St. Tel: (01) 454 5533.
www.aikenpromotions.com

Whelans
Bar downstairs, performance area
upstairs. This place has a great
reputation and has drawn in some very
famous names over the years.
Performances generally start at about
8pm – check the website for what's on,
and to book tickets.
25 Wexford St. Tel: (01) 478 0766.
www.whelanslive.com

Nightclubs

Nightclubs in Dublin seem to take
turns at being the cool place to be.
Most open nightly from about 10pm
until 3am, and have several layers of
activity from chill-out rooms to
cinemas. They have admission charges
of around €10, and drinks are generally
dearer than those in the pubs that
customers have just staggered out of.

Club M
Long-established nightclub with
attached champagne bar. Lots of dark
colours and mood lighting. Look out
for flyers about town for discounted

drinks and reduced admission. Check
the website for what's on.
Cope Street, Temple Bar.
Tel: (01) 671 5274. www.clubm.ie

Lillie's Bordello
Calling itself the most prestigious
nightclub in Dublin, this place gets
loads of B-list stars through its doors,
as well as the occasional big name.
Opulent rooms, live music, open most
nights from 11pm. Be prepared to
queue and be inspected by dress-code
conscious bouncers.
2 Adam Court, Grafton St.
Tel: (01) 679 9204. www.lilliesbordello.ie

Theatres

Dublin has some excellent theatres
and theatre companies, from fringe
theatre to the more mainstream.
Opening in spring 2010 is the shiny
new Grand Canal Theatre, in the
Docklands development project.

Abbey Theatre/Peacock
Showcases new Irish talent.
Lower Abbey St. Tel: (01) 878 7222.
www.abbeytheatre.ie

Bewleys Café Theatre
Daily lunchtime theatre performances
and regular evening performances.
78/79 Grafton Street. Tel: 086 878 4001.
www.bewleyscafetheatre.com

Gate Theatre
European and local playwrights' work.
East Parnell Square. Tel: (01) 874 4045.
www.gate-theatre.ie

The Olympia Theatre
Dublin's oldest theatre.
72 Dame St. Tel: (01) 677 7744.

Accommodation

During the summer and at certain times of the year it can be difficult to obtain accommodation in Dublin, especially in the city centre. Book in advance to avoid disappointment and wasting valuable holiday time looking for accommodation.

Hotels and guesthouses in Ireland operate under a star classification based on a system devised by Bord Failte (the Irish Tourist Board) and the Irish Hotels Federation. The most luxurious hotel is classified as five star (★★★★★), with a comfortable and simple hotel classified as one star (★). For guesthouses, the classification is based on the number of facilities available as well as the overall standard. The classification starts at four star (★★★★) with a whole range of facilities and full restaurant, down to one star (★), which has far fewer facilities. There is a range of online booking services available. The **Irish Hotels Federation** also offers a booking service on its website (*13 Northbrook Rd. Tel: (01) 497 6459. www.irelandhotels.com*). Alternatively, you can contact the hotel directly – many now have their own websites.

Abbey Court Hostel

Kinlay House

Camping

There are two registered campsites in the Dublin area. One is:

Camac Valley Tourist Caravan & Camping Park

Naas Rd, Clondalkin.
Tel: (01) 464 0644.
Fax: (01) 464 0643.
www.camacvalley.com

Youth hostels

An Óige is the Irish Youth Hostel Association. The central Dublin hostel is popular and fills up early during the summer months. It is cheaper if you are a member of the International Youth Hostel Association.

An Óige Dublin International Youth Hostel

Set in an old convent school, this place is roomy with lots of facilities including en-suite private doubles, but is a good walk out of the town centre in a relatively wild part of town.

61 Mountjoy St.
Tel: (01) 830 1766.
Fax: (01) 830 1600.
www.anoige.ie

Hostels (no rating)

There are numerous hostels in the centre of Dublin. Most have the option of beds in a dormitory or double rooms. Some to try include:

Abbey Court Hostel

Very central. Clean, lots of sleeping options including apartments and en-suite doubles, Wi-Fi, kitchen, laundry, and so on. Doubles aren't a lot cheaper than some three-star hotels.

29 Bachelors Walk.
Tel: (01) 878 0700.
www.abbey-court.com

Avalon House

Pleasant hostel, nice private rooms, lots of space. Facilities include its own cinema, and it offers city tours. Centrally located for the Aungier St/South Great George's St pub-crawl area.

55 Aungier St.
Tel: (01) 475 0001.
www.avalon-house.ie

Barnacles Temple Bar House

Small but happening place right in Temple Bar, so you can just fall out of your club and into bed.

19 Temple Lane,
Temple Bar.
Tel: (01) 671 6277.
www.barnacles.ie

Kinlay House

Very central. Can get noisy at night.

Christchurch, 2–12 Lord Edward St.
Tel: (01) 679 6644.
www.kinlayhouse.ie

Litton Lane Hostel

Small, friendly, inexpensive, very central. Sinéad O'Connor once recorded here.

2–4 Litton Lane.
Tel: (01) 872 8389.

Marlborough Hostel

Small, all dorm place with movies and barbecue. Bit of a walk into town.

81–82 Marlborough St.
Tel: (01) 874 7629. www.
marlboroughhostel.com

Inexpensive guesthouses

Bed & Breakfast (B&B) is a great way to experience life in a family home, although the ones in Dublin are more like small hotels. They are mostly in townhouses and are usually slightly cheaper than the more luxurious guesthouses. Some of the better ones include:

Glen Guesthouse ★★

Small, comfortable place with aspirations.

84 Lower Gardiner St.
Tel: (01) 855 1374.
www.glen-guesthouse-dublin.com

Grafton Guest House ★★★

Well-maintained place, close to both Temple Bar and the South Great George's St/Aungier St strip.

26/27 South Great George's St.
Tel: (01) 679 2041. www.
graftonguesthouse.com

Harvey's Guesthouse ★★★

Family-run, a little way out of town.

11 Upper Gardiner St.
Tel: (01) 874 8384. www.
harveysguesthouse.com

Luxury guesthouses

Well-appointed Dublin guesthouses include:

Aberdeen Lodge ★★★★

Great place to stay if nightlife isn't your thing. Quiet area, lots of luxury.

53 Park Avenue,
Ballsbridge.
Tel: (01) 283 8155.
www.aberdeen-lodge.com

Ariel House ★★★★

Classy, quiet place. Off-street parking. Close to DART.

52 Lansdowne Rd.
Tel: (01) 668 5512.
www.ariel-house.net

Glenogra House ★★★★

Another Ballsbridge gem: quiet, close to some good restaurants, the RDS and DART.

64 Merrion Rd,
Ballsbridge.
Tel: (01) 668 3661.
www.glenogra.com

Merrion Hall ★★★★

More a boutique hotel than a guesthouse, this place has some good full-board offers, lots of little luxuries, and guaranteed peace and quiet.

54–55 Merrion Rd,
Ballsbridge.
Tel: (01) 668 1426.
www.merrionhall.com

Number 31 ★★★★

All the luxury of the Ballsbridge places, but more central.
31 Leeson Close.
Tel: (01) 676 5011.
www.number31.ie

Cheaper central hotels

Some of the cheaper central hotels include:

The Castle Hotel ★★
This set of Georgian terraces in a relatively peaceful area offers good value for money. Basic clean rooms, helpful staff, spacious public areas.

2–4 Gardiner Row.
Tel: (01) 874 6949. www.
thecastlehotelgroup.com

Arlington Hotel ★★★
Big, very central place with lots of activities going on at night.
23–25 Bachelors Walk.
Tel: (01) 804 9100.
Email: info@arlington.ie.
www.arlington.ie

Bewley's Ballsbridge ★★★
All the peace and quiet of out of town, plus a good three-star hotel at two-star prices.
Merrion Rd.
Tel: (01) 668 1111. Email:
res@bewleyshotels.com.
www.bewleyshotels.com

Blooms Hotel ★★★
Right in the centre of Temple Bar. Good for partygoers.
Anglesea St. Tel: (01) 671
5622. www.blooms.ie

Jury's Inn Christchurch ★★★
Nice place, like all Jury's; charges a room rate, so good for families or sharing.
Christchurch Place.
Tel: (01) 454 0000.
www.jurysinns.com

Jury's Inn Custom House ★★★
Standard Jury's, set a little out of the way in the Docklands.

The Arlington is a cheaper option right in the heart of the city

Customhouse Quay.
Tel: (01) 854 1500.
info@jurysinns.com.
www.jurysdoylehotels.com

Jury's Inn Parnell Street ★★★

Newly built, comfortable place; all the Jury's benefits. Room-only rates are a great bargain for families.

Moore St Plaza.
Tel: (01) 878 4900.
www.jurysinns.com

Mid-range Hotels

Maldron ★★★

Newly built and straight out of the starting gate, this is efficiently run, friendly and has everything you need for a quiet, comfortable stay in the heart of the city. The restaurant is well worth checking out, too.

Parnell Sq West.
Tel: (01) 871 6800.
www.maldronhotels.com

Mespil Hotel ★★★

Modern, well-run, just outside the noise of the city and close to some of the more fashionable restaurants. Booking five days in advance brings this place down to the budget range.

Mespil Rd.
Tel: (01) 488 4600.
www.mespilhotel.com

Harrington Hall ★★★★

Pretty, Georgian terraced house with its own off-street parking. Centrally located and close to the Luas and Grafton Street.

70 Harcourt Street.
Tel: (01) 475 3497.

The Gresham ★★★★

Lovely old hotel, oozing with history and recently renovated.

23 Upper O'Connell St.
Tel: (01) 874 6881.
www.gresham-hotels.com

The Morgan ★★★★

In the heart of Temple Bar, this is a beautifully designed, ultra-modern, boutique hotel.

10 Fleet St, Temple Bar.
Tel: (01) 643 7000.
www.themorgan.com

The Morrison ★★★★

Classy, stylish place, a little out of the buzz of the city centre with lovely views over the river. Room rate rather than per-person rate makes it good value for a quality place.

Ormond Quay Lower.
Tel: (01) 887 2400.
www.morrisonhotel.ie

Luxury hotels

Luxury city-centre five-star hotels in Dublin include:

Radisson Blu Royal Hotel ★★★★

One of the city's newest kids on the block. Modern and stylish, with all the little luxuries you could ask for. Nice pool.

Golden Lane, Dublin 8.
Tel: (01) 898 2900.
www.radissonblu.ie/
royalhotel-dublin

La Stampa ★★★★

Gorgeous boutique hotel with exotic Mandala Spa and Balzac restaurant.

35–36 Dawson St.
Tel: (01) 677 4444.
www.lastampa.ie

Fitzwilliam Hotel ★★★★★

Conran-designed, Michelin-star restaurant, very central. You'd better have sturdy plastic for this place.

St Stephen's Green.
Tel: (01) 478 7000. Email:
enq@fitzwilliamhotel.com.
www.fitzwilliamhotel.com

The Four Seasons ★★★★★

Gorgeous, purpose-built hotel, with spa, pool, fitness room, all the bars and dining rooms you could ask for. You need never leave the hotel.

Amazing service. In a quiet area of the city, 10 minutes from the centre. *Simmonscourt Road. Tel: (01) 665 4000. www.fourseasons.com*
The Merrion Hotel ★★★★
Posh place with all the little luxuries this price range is able to offer. *21–24 Upper Merrion St. Tel: (01) 603 0600. www.merrionhotel.com*
Radisson Blu St Helen's Hotel ★★★★★
This fabulous hotel has undergone renovation to a very high standard. *Stillorgan Rd. Tel: (01) 218 6000. www.radissonblu.ie/ sthelenshotel-dublin*
The Shelbourne ★★★★★
An old Dublin institution. *27 St Stephen's Green. Tel: (01) 663 4500. www.theshelbourne.ie*

The Maldron hotel in Parnell Square

Practical guide

Arriving
Formalities
Visitors from the UK do not officially require a passport to enter Ireland, but you will need some form of photo identification, so bring a passport anyway. If you are visiting from Australia, the USA, Canada or New Zealand, you will need a passport but not a visa. If you are travelling from other countries, you may need a visa – it is best to check in advance.

By air
Dublin Airport (*Tel: (01) 814 1111. www.dublin-airport.com*) is the country's major international airport and it is about 13km (8 miles) north of the city centre. For information about services at Dublin Airport, flight arrivals and departures, log on to the airport's website. There are a number of ways to get from the airport into the centre of town.

Aircoach Connects the airport with many of the top Dublin hotels and the south side of the city as far as Sandyford. Departs every 10–15 minutes from 5am–midnight and hourly from midnight–5am. Journey time to the airport from the city centre is about 30 minutes. Allow more time at rush hours. Aircoach also have routes from Dublin airport to Cork and Belfast.
Aircoach, Arrivals Level, Dublin Airport, Co. Dublin. Tel: (01) 844 7118. www.aircoach.ie

Airlink Express Dublin bus runs two express bus services to and from the airport. Bus No 747 links the airport with Busaras bus station. Bus No 748 links the major railway stations, Connolly and Heuston, with the airport. The buses run every 15–20 minutes from 7am–11pm.
www.dublinbus.ie

By taxi There is a taxi rank outside the airport. Remember to set a fare before you get in the taxi.

By car The airport is close to the M1 and M50 motorways.

By rail
If you arrive in Dublin by rail you will come into one of two major rail stations close to the centre of the city:

Connolly Station For the arrival of trains from Northern Ireland (including Belfast and Derry) and from Sligo and Wexford (including connections from the ferry terminal at Rosslare Harbour). Ten-minute walk from O'Connell St.

Heuston Station For the arrival of trains from major cities in the Republic of Ireland including Cork, Limerick and Galway. For the city centre take bus 90 or 92 or the Luas to Abbey Street.

By sea
The ports nearest to Dublin are Dublin Port and Dun Laoghaire. Rosslare port is in County Wexford in the Southeast of the country.

Dublin Port Arrivals from Holyhead, Liverpool and the Isle of Man. About 3km (2 miles) from the city centre. Bus No 53 from Busaras (*tel: (01) 872 0000*) to the ferry terminal.
Dublin Port Authority, Alexandra Rd. Tel: (01) 887 6000. Fax: (01) 855 7400. www.dublinport.ie

Dun Laoghaire Ferryport Arrivals from Holyhead. Easy access to the city centre via DART service.
Dun Laoghaire Ferryport, Dun Laoghaire, Co. Dublin. Tel: (01) 204 7700. Fax: (01) 204 7620.

Rosslare Ferryport Ireland's premier ferryport. Arrivals from the Welsh ports Fishguard and Pembroke, and the French ports of Le Havre, Roscoff and Cherbourg. Train service to Connolly Station in Dublin. N11 motorway goes from Dublin to Rosslare.
Rosslare Ferryport, Rosslare Harbour, Co. Wexford. Tel: (053) 913 314. www.irishrail.ie/rosslare/home

Cars and driving

Breakdown

If you are in a hire car, call your hire company if the car breaks down. If not, you can contact a local car breakdown service or get your car towed to the nearest service garage. The **Automobile Association of Ireland** (*56 Drury St. Tel: (01) 617 9999. www.aaireland.ie*) offers breakdown services.

Car hire

There is a wide variety of car hire companies in Ireland and most will have offices at the airport. The majority of hire cars will be manual cars. There are a limited number of automatic cars for hire – you need to book these in advance and they will be more expensive. To get the best deal and guarantee availability, consider booking a car before you leave home. Booking a car on the internet can give considerable savings. To rent a car in Ireland you must be over 21 and under 70 years of age and be able to produce a full valid driving licence from your country of residence. For some companies, you must be over 23. Your licence must be without endorsements and held for at least two years. The usual hire rate quoted will cover third-party/liability insurance, unlimited

Cultural attractions are usually signposted

Practical guide

mileage, VAT and passenger indemnity insurance. It is recommended you take out the additional insurance of a collision damage waiver, so that you are not liable for replacement of the car. If you have an accident, inform the car hire company immediately.

Driving

Driving in Dublin can be a complete nightmare and, although you seem to encounter traffic jams and bad traffic in every major city in the world, they are getting much worse here. You should avoid the rush-hour traffic, which is at its worst during rain and in the winter. Although legally allowed to drink a small amount of alcohol (no greater than 80mg of alcohol per 100ml of blood) and drive in Ireland, you should use public transport, a taxi or walk if you are going to drink.

Fuel

There are plenty of petrol stations in the Dublin area. In every station there are usually unleaded, leaded and diesel pumps. In nearly all service stations you will be able to use your credit card to purchase fuel.

Parking

Finding parking areas in Dublin is difficult. If you do find a parking space, it is likely that you can only leave your car for a maximum of three hours. The parking meters are patrolled by traffic wardens who issue tickets liberally for transgressors, and if you park illegally and do not pay for your parking, your car will be clamped or towed away and you will have to pay to remove it from the pound. If you are only staying in the centre of the city, you should consider not driving and only using public transport. Paying for parking is obligatory Monday–Saturday 7am–7pm and on Sundays in the city centre from 2–6pm. After 8pm, you can pay a parking meter for the first three hours of the following morning.

If you leave your car parked overnight on the street, don't leave any valuables in the vehicle and make sure the alarm is activated. There are various multistorey car parks run by Dublin City Council around the city with security, and it is recommended you park your car in one of these.

Traffic regulations

Drive on the left and use a seatbelt. The speed limits are 112kmph (70mph) on motorways, 96kmph (60mph) on main roads outside built-up areas and 48kmph (30mph) in built-up areas. Carry your driving licence with you at all times. Vehicles towing a caravan or trailer must not exceed 88kmph (55mph) at any time.

Crime

Crime has, in recent years, become a much bigger problem than before. Dublin used to be one of the safest cities to visit in Europe, but this is no longer the case. An increase in drug-related crime is one of the main reasons for this. Be careful at night and perhaps leave some of your valuables in the hotel safe when you go out. Don't carry too much cash when walking around, and avoid going out alone very late at night on badly lit streets with few people about (especially if you are a woman). Your hotel will warn you about particular areas to avoid late at night. Car theft is also a problem so do not leave any valuables in your car.

Customs regulations

Duty free is only available for those who visit Ireland from outside the EU. There are two occasions on which you can purchase duty free. The first is if you are flying directly from Ireland to a non-EU country. The second is if you fly to a non-EU country via an EU country stopover, but you must leave the EU on the same day. If you come from a country in the EU, you are not allowed to buy goods duty free. If you have come from outside the EU you are allowed 200 cigarettes, 2 litres of wine and 1 litre of spirits. The usual customs regulations apply to bringing in banned substances such as contraband, firearms and pornographic material. Particular emphasis is placed on the ban on importing foodstuffs, particularly meat products, in the light of past outbreaks of foot-and-mouth disease and BSE.

CONVERSION TABLE

FROM	TO	MULTIPLY BY
Inches	Centimetres	2.54
Feet	Metres	0.3048
Yards	Metres	0.9144
Miles	Kilometres	1.6090
Acres	Hectares	0.4047
Gallons	Litres	4.5460
Ounces	Grams	28.35
Pounds	Grams	453.6
Pounds	Kilograms	0.4536
Tons	Tonnes	1.0160

To convert back, for example from centimetres to inches, divide by the number in the third column.

MEN'S SUITS

UK	36	38	40	42	44	46	48
Rest of Europe	46	48	50	52	54	56	58
USA	36	38	40	42	44	46	48

DRESS SIZES

UK	8	10	12	14	16	18
France	36	38	40	42	44	46
Italy	38	40	42	44	46	48
Rest of Europe	34	36	38	40	42	44
USA	6	8	10	12	14	16

MEN'S SHIRTS

UK	14	14.5	15	15.5	16	16.5	17
Rest of Europe	36	37	38	39/40	41	42	43
USA	14	14.5	15	15.5	16	16.5	17

MEN'S SHOES

UK	7	7.5	8.5	9.5	10.5	11
Rest of Europe	41	42	43	44	45	46
USA	8	8.5	9.5	10.5	11.5	12

WOMEN'S SHOES

UK	4.5	5	5.5	6	6.5	7
Rest of Europe	38	38	39	39	40	41
USA	6	6.5	7	7.5	8	8.5

Electricity

The standard electrical current is 220/240 volts, and a three-pin square adaptor may be required.

Embassies

American Embassy *42 Elgin Rd. Tel: (01) 668 8777. http://dublin.usembassy.gov*
Australian Embassy *7th Floor, Fitzwilton House, Wilton Terrace. Tel: (01) 664 5300. www.ireland.embassy.gov.au*
British Embassy *29 Merrion Rd. Tel: (01) 205 3700. www.britishembassyinireland.fco.gov.uk*
Canadian Embassy *4th Floor, 65 St Stephen's Green. Tel: (01) 417 4100. www.canada.ie*

Emergency numbers

The free emergency telephone numbers in Ireland are *999* and *112*. You then ask for the emergency service you require: ambulance, police or fire brigade.

Entertainment guides

Many websites and the national newspapers list events in the city.

Look out for *The Ticket* supplement to the *Irish Times* on Thursday, and the *Day and Night* supplement to the *Irish Independent* on Friday for current art and entertainment listings.

Health

Under the EU Reciprocal Medical Treatment Programme, visitors from EU countries are entitled to free medical treatment in Ireland, but should obtain a European Health Insurance Card from their own National Social Security office. In the UK they are available from *www.ehic.org.uk*, by phoning *0845 606 2030*, or from post offices. This should be presented to the doctor if possible before treatment or a consultation starts. Check that the doctor or dentist you visit is registered with the Irish Health Board and tell the office that you want to be treated under the EU social security arrangements. Visitors from countries outside the EU should ensure they have adequate insurance cover before they leave their country of origin. In an emergency, go to the Casualty Department of one of the major Dublin hospitals. The **Eastern Regional Health Authority** (*tel: (01) 679 0700*) will provide information on health services available in the Dublin area. There are three hospitals with an emergency department close to the city centre:
The Mater *Eccles St. Tel: (01) 885 8888.*
St James's Hospital *James's St. Tel: (01) 410 3000.*
Baggot St Hospital *Upr Baggot St. Tel: (01) 668 1577.*

Hiring a bike

Riding a bike is one of the best ways to see Dublin, even if it can sometimes seem a little perilous with all the traffic

Language

Dublin is a bilingual city, but not many people speak Irish and no-one uses it as a first language in the city. Some of the road signs are bilingual and you will even get the odd one just in Irish, so it can be a little confusing when you are driving around the city. Of course, Dubliners all speak very good English; indeed, it has often been said that they speak a better class of English than the English themselves. Many Europeans come to the city to learn English.

Here is a list of Irish words you may come across and their English translations:

An Lár	City centre	**Go raibh maith agat**	Thank you
Baile Atha Cliath	Irish name for Dublin	**Iarnród Éireann**	Irish Rail
Cead Mile Failte	Traditional Irish greeting which means 'one hundred thousand welcomes'	**Mná**	Women, sign on toilets
		Ná Caitear Tobac	Don't smoke
		Ní hea	No
		Oifig an Phoist	Post Office
Dáil	Irish Parliament	**Sea**	Yes
Dia dhuit	Hello	**Sláinte**	Cheers
Fir	Men, sign on toilets	**Stad**	Stop
Garda	Police officer	**Taoiseach**	Irish Prime Minister
Garda Siochána	Police	**An Tuachtaran**	Irish President

Some of the colloquialisms used by Dubliners in their speech are peculiar to the city and you may not understand them. Many are interesting and amusing phrases that you will find yourself using before the end of your visit. Here is a short list of some common slang words you may come across during your stay:

Acting the maggot	Messing	**Gas crack**	Good fun
An awful eejit	Idiot	**Grand day**	Good day, usually means it is not raining
Blatherer	Someone who goes on and on and on	**Having a canary**	A fright
Bleeding deadly	Great	**I will in me hat**	I won't do it
Blow-in	Non-Dubliner who comes to live in the city	**Jacks**	Toilet
		Lashing rain	Heavy rain
Brutal weather	Very bad weather	**Slagging**	Teasing; 'an awful slag' is a term of endearment and not an insult as in Britain
Cheek	Disrespect		
Dote	Nice baby		
Few scoops	A few drinks	**Soft day**	Raining

about. **Dublin Bikes** is the easiest way to try cycling around the city (*www.dublinbikes.ie*).

Insurance

You should take out personal travel insurance from your travel agent, tour operator or insurance company. It should give adequate cover for medical expenses, loss or theft, repatriation, personal liability, third-party motor insurance (but liability arising from motor accidents is not usually included) and cancellation expenses. Always read the conditions, and check that the amount of cover is adequate.

If you hire a car, collision insurance, often called collision damage waiver or CDW, is usually compulsory and charged by the hirer, but it may be as much as 50 per cent of the hiring fee. Check with your own motor insurers before you leave as you may already be covered for CDW on overseas hires by your normal policy. Neither CDW nor your personal travel insurance will protect you from liability arising out of an accident in a hire car, for example, if you damage another vehicle or injure someone. If you are likely to hire a car you should obtain some extra cover, preferably from your travel agent or other insurer before departure.

If you take your own motor vehicle on holiday, check with your motor insurers on your cover for damage, loss or theft of the vehicle, and for liability. A Green Card (third-party cover) is recommended for those from countries outside the EU. The Green Card can be obtained from your local motor insurer. It is not required for those coming from another EU country. It is possible to buy packages providing extra cover for breakdowns and accidents.

Lost property

If you lose some important personal item or it is stolen, report it straight away to the police (*Gardaí*). They will fill out a report and you can then claim the value of the loss from your insurance company. At the airport and at bus and major train stations there will be a lost property office. If you lose something in a supermarket or large retailer, you should go to the customer service desk.

Maps

The Dublin Tourism Centre on Suffolk St has probably the best map of the city centre. For a more detailed map, the *Dublin St Guide* is published by the Ordnance Survey and can be purchased at the **National Map Centre** on Aungier St. *Tel: (01) 476 0471.*

Media

The Irish media is well established and there are some excellent programmes on local television and radio. There are four TV stations: RTE 1, RTE 3, TV3 and the Gaelic channel, TG4 (most but not all of the programmes are in the Irish language). On terrestrial television you can also access the four major British television stations. Most hotels will have satellite TV in the bedrooms. There are more than a few local radio stations (some of them parochial rather than local), including one dedicated to jazz and one to classical music. Talk radio is huge in Ireland and very entertaining. Members of the public phone in and give their passionate opinions about a diverse range of topics, from the terrible traffic problems of the capital to corruption among politicians. Those who phone may even burst into an impromptu song or recite a poem. This makes for amusing entertainment and great radio.

The major national daily newspapers still maintain their literary tradition, and some of Ireland's foremost literary writers feature strongly in the *Irish Times* and *Irish Independent* newspapers. On Sundays, there are the *Sunday Independent* and *Sunday Tribune*, and the British newspaper, *The Sunday Times*, produces an Irish version of its Sunday paper. The *Sunday Business Post*, which focuses on business but also covers other news, may be of interest to those who visit Dublin on business. The largest-selling tabloid newspapers are the Irish versions of English tabloids, *The Irish Sun* and *The Star*. Most newsagents sell English newspapers on the same day as they are issued. For listings of events in Dublin, check the weekly publication *In Dublin* and the monthly *The Dubliner*.

Money matters

The currency in Ireland is the Euro. If you are coming from another country in the EU (with the Euro currency), you will not need to change money. The Euro is divided into 100 cents. There are seven denominations of the Euro note: €5, €10, €20, €50, €100, €200 and €500; and eight denominations of coins: 1 cent, 2 cents, 5 cents, 10 cents, 20 cents, 50 cents and €1 and €2.

Changing money

Thomas Cook has an exchange bureau on St Stephen's Green at 118 Grafton St (*tel: (01) 677 0469*), and at North East St (*tel: (01) 878 3944*). You can also change money at the foreign exchange counter of major banks. Thomas Cook will provide you with a better exchange rate than the hotel in which you are staying and has longer opening hours than banks.

Traveller's cheques are a safe way to carry large amounts of money when you are on holiday. Thomas Cook provides an excellent Traveller's Cheques service and offers a 24-hour refund service if they are lost or stolen (*tel: 0044 1733 31 8950 and reverse the charges*).

Credit cards

All major credit cards are accepted at most hotels, restaurants and shops in Dublin. If you lose your credit card or it is stolen, it is best to inform your credit card company immediately.

Pharmacies

There are plenty of pharmacies (called chemists by locals) in the city centre, and they are identified by their distinctive green cross sign. Most Irish pharmacists are highly qualified and give good advice on minor ailments and first aid and can provide a range of over-the-counter (OTC) drugs without a prescription. This may preclude a visit to a general practitioner. Chemists in the city centre with late-night openings include: **O'Connells Late Night Pharmacy**, which has many chains throughout the city centre including Grafton St, O'Connell St and Henry St. The latest opening is 10pm at the branch at 55–56 Lower O'Connell St. **Hamilton Long Late Night Pharmacy** is open until 9pm at 4 Merrion Rd, Ballsbridge and 5pm at O'Connell St. If you are looking for a late-night chemist, there is usually a list of the nearest ones in the window of any chemist.

Police

The Irish police force is called the Garda Siochána (often called the Guards in English, but you will be best understood if you simply call them the police). The Gardaí are very approachable on the streets of Dublin, and are usually happy to help tourists with directions or any other information you require. The nearest Garda Station to the city centre is at Pearse St (near College Green), *tel: (01) 666 9500*.

Post offices

Opening hours for post offices are Monday–Friday 9am–6pm; major post offices also open on Saturdays 10am–1pm. Two centrally located post offices are the historical General Post Office (GPO) on O'Connell St and the Post Office on Suffolk St (opposite Dublin Tourism offices). The GPO has longer opening hours: Monday–Saturday 8am–8pm and Sundays noon–6.30pm.

Public Holidays

The Irish Annual Public Holidays are:
1 January New Year's Day
17 March or the following Monday if it falls on a weekend St Patrick's Day
First Monday in May May Bank Holiday
First Monday in June June Bank Holiday
First Monday in August August Bank Holiday
First Monday in October October Bank Holiday
25 December Christmas Day
26 December St Stephen's Day
Movable feasts are Good Friday and Easter Monday.

Public transport
DART (Dublin Area Rapid Transport)
This electric suburban railway runs from Howth or Malahide, in the northern suburbs of Dublin, as far as Greystones in County Wicklow. Trains run every 15–20 minutes during the day and every 5 minutes during the rush hour. The trains can get full

during rush hour. Last DART leaves the city centre at 11.30pm.

For information call the Rail Travel Centre, tel: (01) 836 6222. www.dart.ie

Dublin Bus:

Routes run from 6am until about 11.30pm (last buses leave the city centre at this time) throughout the city. There is a limited nightlink service that runs on certain routes.

For further information and a complete guide to the bus service and timetables for individual routes contact Dublin Bus, 58 Upper O'Connell St. Tel: (01) 873 4222 (Mon–Sat 9am–5.30pm). Email: info@dublinbus.ie. www.dublinbus.ie. Office open: Mon 8.30am–5.30pm, Tue–Fri 9am–5.30pm, Sat 9am–1pm. Closed: Sun & public holidays.

Luas

The Luas (Irish for 'speed') is a light rail system serving Dublin. There are two lines – the green and the red. The green line connects Sandyford to St Stephen's Green. The red line connects Tallaght to Connolly. *Tel: 1800 300 604. www.luas.ie*

Outside Dublin

For further information about train or bus journeys outside Dublin, contact **Iarnroid Eireann** (*tel: (01) 836 6222. www.irishrail.ie*) or **Bus Eireann** (*tel: (01) 836 6111. www.buseireann.ie*).

Religious worship

There are plenty of churches in Dublin. The main religion is Roman Catholicism but there are also Protestant churches. Your hotel will provide you with information about Sunday service times.

Senior citizens

There are various discounts available for senior visitors to Dublin. There is free travel if you are over 65 years of age and you will get free or reduced admission into museums. You will need identification to prove your age.

Student and youth travel

If you are under 18 you are entitled to reduced fares when you travel on public transport. You will need to prove your age with some form of identification card.

If you are a student with a student card (e.g. the International Student Identity Card), you can purchase a Travelsave Stamp from the student travel company **USIT**, which gives travel discounts on public transport in Ireland and on Irish Ferries.

USIT, 19–21 Aston Quay. Tel: (01) 602 1904. www.usit.ie

Sustainable tourism

Thomas Cook is a strong advocate of ethical and fairly traded tourism and believes that the travel experience should be as good for the places visited as it is for the people who visit them. That's why we firmly support The Travel Foundation, a charity that develops solutions to help improve and protect holiday destinations, their environment, traditions and culture. To find out what you can do to make a positive difference to the places you travel to and the people who live there, please visit *www.thetravelfoundation.org.uk*

Taxis

Taxis can be hailed on the street or at special taxi ranks. Three of the major ranks are at St Stephen's Green, College Green (in front of Trinity College) and O'Connell St. The best way to get a taxi is to phone for one from where you are leaving. Your hotel or restaurant will do this for you, but if you are in a bar you will have to do it yourself.

Telephones

Most telephone numbers in the Dublin area have seven digits with *01* as the prefix. The code for Ireland is *353* if you are dialling Dublin from abroad. Public phone booths are found all over the city. They accept coins, phone cards and you can use your credit card in some. For directory enquiries within Ireland, dial *11811*. For international enquiries, dial *11818*.

Time

Ireland maintains Greenwich Mean Time, but timekeeping and punctuality have never been a characteristic of the Irish. You are likely to have to wait with a smile for what you want. Clocks go forward by 1 hour in mid-March and back 1 hour at the end of October.

Toilets

There are very few public toilet facilities in Dublin. The best approach is to use the toilet in a bar, which you can usually do without having to buy a drink. If the bar is empty it is polite to ask the bartender first. A restaurant is unlikely to be so obliging, and there may be signs saying toilets are only for use by customers.

Tourist information

For tourist information about Ireland, there are two tourist bodies. **Tourism Ireland** provides information for visitors from abroad – their website is *www.tourismireland.com*. Tourism Ireland's brief is the whole island of Ireland. **Fáilte Ireland** provides tourist information about the Republic of Ireland for tourists who are already in Ireland. Their website is *www.ireland.ie*

Visit Dublin
Suffolk Street. Tel: (01) 605 7700. www.visitdublin.com

Tourism Ireland (Australia)
Level 5, 36 Carrington St, Sydney, NSW 2000. Tel: (061) 292 996 177. Fax: (061) 292 996 323.

Tourism Ireland (Canada)
2 Bloor St West, Suite 3403, Toronto, ON M4W 3E2. Tel: 1 416 925 6368. Fax: 1 416 925 6033.

Tourism Ireland (UK)
Nations House, 103 Wigmore St, London W10 1QS. Tel: (020) 7518 0800. Email: info.gb@tourismireland.com. www.tourismireland.com

Tourism Ireland (USA)
345 Park Avenue, 17th Floor, New York NY 10154. Tel: 800 223 6470. Fax: 1 212 371 9052. www.discoverireland.com/us

Visit Dublin is certainly your best bet for information about the city. They also sell tickets for several tours and the very worthwhile Dublin Pass, which, once purchased, allows free access to most of the city's sights.

Travellers with disabilities

Not everywhere in Dublin is accessible for people with disabilities who require a wheelchair. The newer buildings are nearly all wheelchair accessible, but the older the building the less likely this is. In the museums it can be a problem, but the ground floors are accessible in most cases and the more modern museums and galleries, such as Collins Barracks, are totally wheelchair accessible. Dublin Buses have low-floor, fully accessible buses and it is relatively easy to get on and off. For information about sporting facilities in Dublin, contact the **Irish Wheelchair Association**, *Aras Chuchulain, Blackheath Drive, Clontarf. Tel: (01) 818 6428. www.iwa.ie* or **Ableize**, a UK organisation dedicated to resources for those with disabilities. Its website has links to several Irish organisations. *www.ableize.com.* For a taxi service, try **Dublin Wheelchair Taxi Service**, *15 Slademore Drive. Tel: 087 243 1470. www.dublinwheelchairtaxi.com*

Weather

Ireland has a temperate climate and the major influence on the country's weather is the North Atlantic Drift, which is more commonly known as the Gulf Stream. This warm surface ocean current originates in the Gulf of Mexico and produces a mild and humid stream of air, so the temperatures are much milder in the winter than you might expect, considering the city's latitude. You might expect some Canadian winters in Ireland if it were not for the Gulf Stream. There are no extremes of temperature and the rainfall is also pretty consistent throughout the year. The weather is slightly better in Dublin than in some other parts of the country, but it still gets more than its fair share of rain. Global warming may stem the effect of the Gulf Stream, and colder weather may be on the way for Ireland in the distant future.

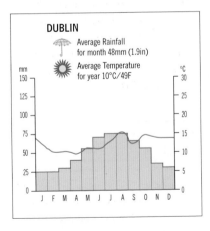

DUBLIN

Average Rainfall for month 48mm (1.9in)

Average Temperature for year 10°C/49F

WEATHER CONVERSION CHART

25.4mm = 1 inch

$°F = 1.8 × °C + 32$

Index